Sabbatical

Sabbatical

A novel

By

N. L. Brisson

This is a work of fiction. Although the characters may resemble real people, the descriptions, dialogue, and situations come from the author's imagination.

Copyright © 1988, 2000 by N. L. Brisson

ISBN: 1-58820-285-2

This book is printed on acid free paper.

1stBooks - rev. 10/27/00

This book is dedicated to my family and friends in gratitude for their love and support.

1
Syracuse

It didn't snow in Syracuse that January, which if you know Syracuse, is unusual. If it had been snowing Danielle probably would not have left in the Toyota on that Wednesday morning. And if she hadn't left that morning she probably wouldn't have gone at all. But winter was late and that fact set off the whole chain of events.

Danielle Giroux was going through a bad time in her life. She was afraid of choking to death. She had dreams about Mama Cass dying with chicken salad blocking her windpipe. She couldn't eat solid food. She was living on Stouffer's spinach souffle and Carnation Instant Breakfast. She was having dreams of her sister who broke her neck in a fatal car accident with her babies in the back seat. She chewed her food thirty-two times and it still wouldn't go down. Her food was cut in tiny pieces. She felt like she was starting over. Danielle dreamed of her mother's younger sister who locked herself in the garage with the car on leaving five children motherless. She felt asphyxiated.

But she went anyway. On a Wednesday in January, fear clutching at her throat, she packed the back seat with everything that would fit and set out on 81 South - first page of the triple A triptik. You can't take Spinach Souffle in the car but she had plenty of Instant Breakfast.

• • • • •

Danielle worried all the way to Scranton about the Poconos. She was petrified that there would be snow in the Poconos. Those curving, dipping, climbing mountain roads - were miraculously clear. She kept going.

• • • • •

Danielle worked as an assistant professor of Early Childhood Education at a small community college near Syracuse. After seven years of teaching she applied for a sabbatical leave to get her master's degree. She only applied to sunny places. She was tired of shoveling snow on to snow banks taller than herself, of having her lips freeze together, of piling on sweaters, boots, coats, gloves, hats, scarves and still having stiff-with-cold toes and fingers for six months of the year. When she saw *Dr. Zhivago* the thing she remembered most was the gloves that Lara wore with the fingers cut out so she could still write. She always thought she would get a pair for when she marked her papers.

Danielle's best friends in Syracuse were Audrey Ann Baker "A-A" and Nicole LeCroix. A-A had a virtual halo of fire-red hair, long and rippled, billowing around her head. She was a big girl, not beautiful, but unique. She could croon and moan just like Janis Joplin, not on **Mercedes Benz**, but on **Piece of My Heart,** scratchy whiskey voice soulfully rendered. Audrey Ann had never worked except once at General Electric for a couple of years; she survived because she was a born entertainer, with a lively, creative and independent spirit. People just loved to have her around.

Nicole, on the surface, was an "air head". Petite, brunette and pretty, she was the one of the three who the men called out to and followed. Her favorite sayings were "never pick your face on a Friday" and "you never know who you're going to meet." She had great style and looked wonderful in clothes. Better yet she was confident about her looks, which would probably have been enough even in the absence of beauty. But there was more to Nicole than it seemed at first. She too was an adventurer and a quester after experience, knowledge and wisdom.

Danielle was the kind of girl who people said had "a pleasant face." She was very short and sturdily built with a

2

few sexy curves thrown in so that it wasn't a total loss. She had dirty blonde hair that she occasionally tried to change to true blonde with varying degrees of success. She had chin length thick hair which was usually permed and left to dry *au naturel* in an unruly mass of chunky curls. Danielle was anything but stylish and sure of herself; always self-conscious around men. Danielle was the only one of the three with a college education. She was an avid reader and knew a bit about art (who's he", her father always said) and music. She had a little common sense, no sense of adventure, but enough curiosity so that she almost always went along with the plans of A-A and Nicole.

They were an unlikely trio (Danielle was often involved in trios, probably because she grew up with two sisters). Danielle met Nicole first. It was during her first year of teaching. Danielle answered an ad in the **Post-Standard** for a roommate. Nicole was one of the girls who lived in the apartment. Each had something the other craved. Nicole; the style, the technique of being social, which Danielle lacked. Danielle had the education that Nicole was fascinated by. So they teamed up. Their first trip of many was to Penn State to visit Danielle's roommate from college. Nicole lost a heel; Charles Lloyd breathed on their necks. It was enough. They were hooked on wandering. They went shopping, they went to parties, they went to the bars. Nicole flirted her way innocently through the Syracuse nights. Danielle watched, marveled, and learned. Nicole also watched Danielle. She decided if Danielle could go to college anyone could. So she went to the State University and drifted in and out of Danielle's life for the next four years.

When Nicole left Danielle had a new roommate, Amanda, a very tiny girl with long blonde swinging hair and a very serious approach to life. She was an extremely intellectual girl, a philosopher, a seeker after spiritual truth. She was also a seeker after men. She looked for a "true" relationship which perhaps existed only in her abstractions.

She seemed able to do with men as she pleased, except one, a teacher at the college where she worked with Danielle. Jeremy Johns, (you always said his two names together) seemed the perfect match for Amanda, but where she was definite, he was vague. He was a lovely man, a spiritual man; where Amanda had two feet planted firmly on the ground; Jeremy Johns floated somewhere between Milton's angels and Dante's poor tormented souls.

• • • • •

It was still daylight...the Poconos still iceless. Danielle moved through the bare winter mountains lost in her memories.

• • • • •

Through Amanda, Danielle met a whole group of young faculty from the college, mostly men. It was the 70's; rock music, wine, marijuana, social consciousness, communal spirit, and women's lib. But Amanda needed Jeremy, so women's lib notwithstanding, her pursuit of the man led to endless parties with Jeremy Johns and all his friends. Sex, booze and smoke saturated the atmosphere every night from dinnertime until four a.m. Danielle tagged along and swam with the rest in the steamy nightlong vigils. Not much in the way of sex actually happened for anyone but Amanda. Everyone else sublimated, they drank more wine, smoked more pot, ate more food and communicated all their hot vibrations, Danielle imagined, through the German Shepherd dog, Jason. Jason didn't seem to mind. He was a wonderful conductor, letting the electrical current pass through with a placid air of contentment. Smart dog, he got more physical affection than anyone and he didn't seem to notice that the current only passed through on its way elsewhere.

They all truly loved each other for that time because they made each other happy. Each one had an instrument and they played and sang along with the songs they listened to. Danielle played the tambourine. They sounded wonderful. Judy Collins sang **Song for Judith.** To them Judy was just an incidental, although perfect, voice added to their harmonies. They were "the Band." They sang **The Boxer,** Simon and Garfunkel weren't even there. It was Danielle and her friends, they were the stars. For those moments they felt so close, like a family, like Danielle's original family, totally asexual by then, incest taboo. By morning the feeling would pass and a certain strangeness would set in until the next night when the whole "trip" would happen all over again. For once Nicole, away at school, was jealous of Danielle's social life. She would come to town on the weekend and try to understand, but she had her own life and was on a different wavelength for a while.

During the time with Amanda Westfall and Jeremy Johns, Danielle met Audrey Ann of the red hair. Audrey was an older student of the community college. The powerful magnet of drug-induced love drew A-A whose natural warmth survived best in a steamy environment. Also she loved a good time and a good man (although she was too Catholic to feel really comfortable with the sexual revolution). She moved in with Amanda and Danielle and shared the rent. She transferred to SU. She was a psychology major. Amanda, Danielle and A-A sat around their kitchen when each night was over drinking herb tea and analyzing, sifting all the feeling, motivations, interactions and personalities, trying to nail things down, to explain things, to "know" the meaning of life. Nicole sometimes joined the informal group therapy sessions, eating the cheese blintzes and adding a point. She was a pragmatist and could not believe how difficult they made simple things, but they eventually converted her so she could see how truly complicated simple things really are.

5

· · · · ·

Wilkes Barre, Williamstown, Hazelton, Danielle passed the towns on Route 81 South, going through the Poconos. Her memories tempered her fears.

· · · · ·

Summer - Nicole and Audrey Ann were out of school. They took their act on the road, once again seeking warmth and, although only Nicole would admit it, men. They packed a tent, three sleeping bags, camp stove and clothes; they were off to Cape Hatteras and Ocracoke. They went in Danielle's car; Danielle and Nicole took turns driving. Audrey Ann had never renewed her driver's license. Danielle drove without fear in those days, not well, but without white knuckles and heart palpitations. It took fifteen hours to get there, straight through except one stop for dinner. Danielle loved food and as yet had no trouble swallowing it. They had hush puppies, the sweet kind, not the onion kind. They took pictures of each other behind a little empty stand called The Clamdigger, nowhere near a beach. By the time they got to the Outer Banks it was blackest night. They didn't even have night like that in Syracuse. Danielle was driving, all three were bitchy, Danielle haranguing every time a car passed that the camp sites would all be full, Nicole and A-A jeering her on. Danielle also believed that they were on a thin highway with the ocean lapping on either side of them. If was a reasonable belief for someone who had crossed the Chesapeake Bay Bridge for the first time and who couldn't see a thing due to pitch darkness with a little night blindness thrown in. But Nicole and Audrey Ann did not share this belief either. Danielle pulled into what she thought was the camp site carefully trying to avoid the ocean encroaching on either side, beyond rationality, dead beat and lost on this imagined landscape. The tires spun in the soft sand, they were up to the hubcaps. Now Danielle saw the last campsite disappearing with every set of taillights that passed. Nicole and A-A rolled their eyes and looked for cardboard or wood to put under the tires. They pitched their tent in the glow of their car headlamps. When they woke up at their campsite in the morning they were inexplicably surrounded by only a handful of people. Danielle knew all the others had slinked off early. Nicole and A-A exchanged looks and snickered and they all packed up their gear. They took the Ferry from Hatteras to Ocracoke. Their tent was in the dunes right next to the beach, one dollar a night. The price was right, the neighborhood the best. Nicole was, of course, the only one who met a man. She, in fact, met two, brothers, who owned a charter fishing boat. Handsome young wild men with deep tans and devilish smiles. Every morning they tried to catch the ferry in time so Nicole could go out with "the fleet". Every morning, weary-eyed, they were the first ones in line at the ferry landing. By the time they made the crossing the boat was always out to sea already. Finally they left the sandy dunes and the glowing green phosphorescent animals that stuck to their feet along with the grains of sand and moved to Buxton, just above Hatteras. Nicole stayed up all night partying with her two beaus. Audrey Ann and Danielle watched sport fishing films at the country club, also at the invitation of Nicole's sibling rivals. Nicole finally did get to go out on the boat that next morning, but the combination of no sleep and too much chemical stimulation forced her to abandon her bikini for the head and the bed. Audrey Ann fell in love too, with a guy in Buxton, but as usual, she loved from afar. Although they sang a million choruses of "Goin' to Buxton", they never even spoke to this young surfer. Danielle, still too shy to flirt, just looked on and enjoyed (and envied).

Through the Poconos, still in Pennsylvania, the day wore on. Danielle drove steadily south with her thoughts.

*   *   *   *   *

Danielle and A-A still lived in the big old flat, scene of all the kitchen conversations. Amanda didn't live there with them now. She had joined a commune of Sufis and had a new name that no one could pronounce. Their new roommate was a young guy, Todd, a construction worker; nice enough, but not a romantic interest. Danielle's parents didn't understand, the arrangement upset them, but Danielle and Audrey Ann felt very liberated even though they still somehow ended up doing most of the cleaning, then all of the cleaning.

Danielle and A-A went occasionally to a small bar called "The Barge". It was full of college types and laborers mixed. Things started out quietly, gradually increased in intensity, often ended in fistfights that exploded out into the street. Danielle and Audrey Ann were with friends, they were drinking, they were talking and laughing, but all Danielle saw was the tall, loose-limbed auburn-haired guy with the emaciated body, Christ's face and Warren Beatty's grin staring at her from the next table. His name was Leonard, Len, and he was doing construction but he was really an artist he said. They started to see each other regularly. Danielle was convinced that he would be a great artist, so was Len. He was a madman, he loved to howl like a wolf, he wore a long black cape, he lived in a tenement. He was writing a play. He was a voracious lover, he never did get real satisfaction, exhaustion usually won out first. They read Shakespeare together, taking parts. His spelling was a foreign language; his play was either a great esoteric work of art or trash. Danielle wasn't sure. Nicole came home for the summer and started going out with Len's friend, Perry. Perry was a tall, thin guy too. He was wonderfully attractive, probably raised in a warm, loving country-club-going, tennis-playing family. He was real and charming. The four of them spent the summer following Len around. He needed a lead character for his play, only Nicole would do. Danielle, he said, had a peasant face, not aristocratic like his. Danielle was insulted but secretly agreed. He filmed Nicole at Butternut Creek with a video camera - she was the lady in distress, cringing against the rock, ready to leap to her death. He was the vampire perching on rocks with his dangerous eyes threatening over the edge of his cape.

Summer ended, Nicole went back to school. Len wanted to go to Paris to study painting. He didn't want a permanent relationship. Danielle pretended that she didn't either; she could see that constancy would never be Len's forté

Danielle was home one day with Audrey Ann and Todd. Todd was recovering from surgery. Len came sweeping in wearing his vampire cape. Danielle and Len curled up together on the couch to watch television, a rare occurrence as vampire artists seldom curl up on couches or watch TV. Todd was pacing, complaining of pains in his lower back. He asked Danielle if she would rub liniment on his back. She didn't really want to but it seemed the only humane thing to do. Todd, for some reason clear only to Freud, exposed his nether cheeks during the procedure. Danielle ignored his behavior, decided not to make a big deal of it and rubbed in the liniment. Len exploded, unfolding his bony limbs, knocking over the coffee table and its contents. He accused her of promiscuity, of at the very least stupidity (probably closer to the truth). He, even so, felt moved to defend his male honor or her female honor or at least she thought honor was involved. He grabbed Todd by his pajama top lapels (luckily his buns were by now tucked away), ripped him off his feet straight from the rocking chair, punched him in mid air. Todd, in the middle of his slightly hypochondriacal recuperation was too stunned to defend himself. Besides self-defense would have been out of character in the role he was playing at the moment. Perhaps she wasn't being fair. Some pain was probably still involved in all that sudden physical contortion and after all the punch probably did hurt. For whatever reason Todd couldn't make the transition from invalid to pugilist. Danielle defended him, sending Len out into the street black cape flying. Len apologized but now she suspected he might not be a great artist, only a madman.

They kept seeing each other, Danielle, still shy, was not confident enough to start over; Len, perhaps, wanted to be saved. She found out she was pregnant. She talked with Len about it. She didn't want to marry him, she was beginning to see him as he "really" was, rather than as Vincent Van Gogh in *Lust for Life*. She began to suspect that he was neither an artist, nor a madman; he was an alcoholic. She mentioned abortion. He was violently against it.

She was at work when her brother called. She had an instant premonition that this would be terrible news. She was right. Her sister was dead, her car slid into a parked truck on a snowy, slippery winter day. She was dead when she arrived at the hospital. Her neck was broken.

There was a gasoline shortage. Danielle had to call the police to find a place to get gas, it was an even day and she had an odd numbered license plate. She had to sign for the gas; they gave her just enough to get to her parents' house outside the city.

Her parents were devastated. Danielle was ill. The morning sickness was so bad that she didn't know how she would make it through the funeral. She had been vomiting constantly for days, a spastic stomach the doctor said. He gave her Dramamine. Miraculously the vomiting stopped for the three days of the funeral. Her abortion was scheduled for the first day of the wake. She thought about divine justice, discarded the idea. She canceled the appointment. She had to pick out an outfit for Laura to wear. She did it in a daze; it made no sense to her whatever. It made her believe in God again.

Len never showed up; he called, said he couldn't handle it and he was sorry, goodbye. When she lost the baby, she knew she was through with Len forever. He left for Paris soon after. Danielle couldn't cry anymore, ever, not even over sad movies, not even over sad days. The only thing that made her cry was having to do something she knew she couldn't do, shouldn't have to do all by herself. Self-pity was the only thing that could still do the trick.

· · · · ·

She was through Pennsylvania, into Virginia, into the South. She had the rhythm of traveling now. She felt more confident. She had picked out a motel to stay at in Virginia. It was just beginning to be dusk.

2
Virginia

Danielle was growing impatient for the sign announcing her exit. It was getting darker. She was getting scared again. She saw a tractor-trailer jack-knifed on the grassy divide. She shook off her panic and drove on, a little slower, hair on her arms on end, tingling. She saw another jack-knifed tractor-trailer. It took Danielle a while to realize that a very fine mist was falling, that the southern temperature had dropped, that the mist was freezing in thin, thin layers on this southern highway; impossible to see. She was paralyzed, her only thought, "get off the highway." She took the next exit, didn't even look at the route number or name. Danielle realized her error, the back roads were worse than the highway. She crawled along; her tires sliding precariously, each ditch a possible disaster. It was a country road, very dark, no street lamps, few houses, lots of ditches. She pulled into a driveway at the top of a hill. It was a long drive, the house sat way back, a homey yellow light showing through the living room curtains. She felt abandoned, even though she knew she had made the choice to travel. She was angry at Audrey Ann, she was angry at Nicole. They really had abandoned her to this deadly fate on a backcountry road in Virginia.

•   •   •   •   •

Nicole was in love, for real this time with David Mofson. Danielle loved him too. Nicole needed someone to settle her down. David was just the man for the job. He was handsome and bright, but with a serious nature and strong sense of responsibility. But why did they have to live in Miami? Danielle and Nicole had been fighting a lot before Nicole left, but Nicole was like Danielle's sister, they were family squabbles, arising out of the phase where friends have gotten to know each other's idiosyncrasies but have not yet accepted them. A typical fight -- Nicole's niece made her confirmation. Danielle agreed to make an antipasto for the reception. But Nicole just had to go to this house sale. So did ninety-nine other people. Nicole had to take a number and stand in line. Danielle went home to make her salad. By the time they arrived at the reception with the fifteen-dollar salad everyone had already eaten. Danielle was livid; Nicole was not contrite. -- But now that Nicole was gone Danielle felt deserted by her. There was no one to fill the gap.

Audrey Ann left next to go cross country financed by a settlement she received for broken bones, a car knocked her down on her way to classes. Now recovered, but with some permanent knee damage, she got a driver's license and a car, found an old friend's daughter who was also heading west and off they went. Audrey Ann had addresses all across the country and back, she never had to stay in a hotel once, although she did camp out a few times on the way (she didn't know anyone who knew anyone in Iowa or Nebraska.) Danielle kept track of her travels through post cards and news flashes from A-A's family or other mutual friends. Now she was in San Francisco, now in Tucson, now in Sante Fe, now in Texas. Always somewhere far away.

Danielle rationalized her loneliness. It was good for the three of them. They had grown too close, too similar. The threesome was too safe, sort of another womb they had wandered into, found cushy and occupied on a semi-permanent basis. She reasoned this would give them a chance to grow as individuals. But she felt like an amputee, a Siamese triplet surgically divided and set out on her own. She didn't know how to start. She needed someone to "hash things over" with. Where were those two when you needed them?

She went on teaching. She moved in with her younger sister, Lily, and realized she didn't know her very well and that she was a rather nice person with her own hopes and hang-ups. She decided to go back to school. That was when she decided to get a sabbatical and do school all at once, in one year. It was hard to get a master's degree part time. That was when she started applying to sunny places: Miami, Tucson, clinging unconsciously to Nicole and Audrey Ann. Audrey Ann loved Tucson. She told Danielle that if Danielle went there to school she would go with her, meet her on the way and they could go out there. That was how they planned it. But it took almost two years to get the sabbatical, clear the way through entanglements and finally pack things in boxes and knapsacks ready to go. By then Danielle couldn't eat solid food. She believed in death. By then A-A had fallen in love with a young boy in one of her classes at a special school for emotionally disturbed children. A-A couldn't go to Tucson; John was now her foster son and she couldn't leave the state of Florida, as he wasn't released by his parents. Danielle was happy for her, but now she had to travel all alone, in January, by herself, cross-country to Tucson. She couldn't back out now, the papers were all signed, a new teacher hired to take her place, the new Toyota in her parking lot.

· · · · ·

So it was Audrey's Ann's fault that Danielle was sitting here, somewhere in Virginia, at night, in the freezing rain, waiting for someone to save her, all alone, with no hope of rescue. Mom! Ha. Mom couldn't even drive, what could she do? She could tell Dad to come get her. In Virginia, in the middle of the darkness, in the freezing rain. Not possible.

She couldn't go on. She cried this time, not grief still, but definitely self-pity. How could her mother have let her go? She collected herself a little, after all she couldn't sit forever in a stranger's driveway and she hadn't really expected her parents to save her for a number of years now. She had to go down that hill and the next one. She gathered whatever little bit of courage she had and slid on down. At the bottom of the hill was her motel.

The desk clerk probably thought she was a nut case, but he had rooms and he couldn't turn her out on a night like this. Her hands shook as she signed the register. She went to the restaurant and ordered a dinner that she knew she couldn't eat. Then she went to sleep without a thought for the next day.

• • • • •

Danielle had not always been like this. She had not always approached life with fear flags flying. Until she had that sudden realization that people die; not only when they're old, their life a circle, complete and full; but anytime, in an unsuspecting moment, life's circle barely begun. Before she knew that, she had approached life like a dessert tray, with delight, if not always good sense. I'll have one of these, and one of these. Now she realized life was really more like sitting down to endless meals of that Japanese fish, fugu, the one that could kill you if it hadn't been cleaned right; each time the question; good chef or bad? Good day or bad? She hated the uncertainty of it. She knew the danger was supposed to improve the pleasure, but for her it didn't. She wanted the security of her preawakened consciousness back. She wanted to know that we all face death, but she wanted to know it as she had, only with her head, not with her heart (or whatever part of us it was that made us know something with every fiber of our being.) Her new awareness made Danielle feel tired, exhausted. It made her feel so weary with living that for a while she could not imagine going on. And right now she really wasn't. She didn't know why she was going to Tucson, or graduate school. She did it automatically because it was the next thing on the list; the plans were already in the works. But it was no longer a cream puff or a Napoleon. It

16

was all that damn Japanese fish, over and over again. These were Danielle's thoughts as she got ready to hit the road again the next morning

3
Tennessee

Danielle drove steadily southwest the next day. By the time she left the hotel all of the ice had already melted from the roads. They were dry. And although the day was overcast, she was rested and had that confidence that came to her with each new day. She was not a grudge holder. She felt that the worst was over. After all God knew she was scared and alone. Surely he would reroute future weather systems, mountain ranges, criminals, pimps and other unimaginable hazards. Danielle also did not really believe that God in any way meddled in everyday human affairs. She never reconciled the behavior and the belief. She appealed to God just in case.

Danielle had never driven this far from Syracuse along this particular route before. She was scared of the Poconos because she knew they were there. If she had known what was ahead she might have turned back, but she didn't so she drove through the rest of Virginia alternately daydreaming and listening to the radio. She didn't notice the surrounding countryside much. It was January and dreary. She was more aware of the trajectory of the highway.

• • • • •

Her thoughts this day were of her sister, Laura. Laura was the first child in the family of four. Danielle knew that Laura had had it hardest of all of them. She was the pioneer child. She grew into each stage first and had to pave the way.

Laura was always a small girl. She had been born premature and took a long time to catch up. She was a thin child with red rimmed eyes and a pale face, fragile looking, but not unhealthy. Danielle's mother favored her a little because she had come so close to losing her. Danielle's mother said that Danielle used to follow the two of them around the house biting the backs of their legs. Danielle still felt guilty about that. She felt guilty about a lot of things when she thought about Laura.

She felt guilty about the clothes she used to sneak out of her sister's closet and wear to school. She also felt embarrassed that she had almost always been caught before she could smuggle them back in. Sometimes she had even left the clothes in a heap on the chair in their room. It seemed petty to be bothered by this and if Laura were still here they would probably have laughed about it some day. But now it was one more piece of unfinished business between them, and it could never be mitigated by future actions.

She felt guilty that she didn't know her sister better. They grew up in the same house after all. It seemed that she couldn't remember any specific incidents in which they had shared a real closeness. Well maybe one, they had used to lie on their backs in their beds in their attic room. The ceiling was made of plywood boards painted white and separated by white molding. They would fantasize floor plans on the ceiling; living room over here, kitchen off the living room, all big rooms, lots of space. Unlike the house they grew up in. Totally.

Laura had grown into a pretty teenager by then, Danielle an awkward preteen, always just one year behind chronologically. Laura showed promise of boyfriends, marriage. Danielle, already sure no one would really fall in love with her, unable to imagine being part of a couple, shocked all of the neighbors by saying she planned to wear a black velvet wedding dress with mint green trim, that she would have a chocolate wedding cake.

Laura did well in high school, she got the award for Latin, her name was on a plaque there. She was the president of her sorority. That was the only reason Danielle got in. They had to pledge sisters. She had to peel oranges for football players, dress like a frog and croak, pass out gum to members, wear 21 pigtails in her hair with her socks rolled down to her ankles. Danielle wasn't proud of what she had done to become a member, but once you were in, belonging to sorority was like having another family, albeit, all female.

Laura was organized and planned things consciously. She did not leave home to go to college. She went for two years to the same community college where Danielle now taught. Laura got a job and then she got married. Danielle rarely saw her. When she did her sister seemed like a magazine page. Her hair was always done, it was frosted blonde, and she often wore a hair band. It was sprayed so every hair was in place. Her outfits were always coordinated and had a somewhat confined, but elegant look. Actually she looked similar to the way Jackie Kennedy looked, always meticulous. Laura made matching outfits for herself and her baby daughter. But Danielle didn't know who Laura was, what she wanted, really wanted. Perhaps Laura never had a chance to find out herself, or perhaps she already had it. No matter, Danielle missed her, and felt Laura was cheated, cheated out of watching her two little daughters grow up. Danielle used to try to send her little posthumous bulletins about her daughters' progress from time to time.

●　●　●　●　●

Virginia changed to Kentucky. Danielle turned on the radio. She wished she hadn't. They were predicting a terrible ice storm from Memphis to the middle of Texas. Now Danielle realized that she had been thinking; that she had been derelict in her duty. If she hadn't been thinking, if she had been paying attention, this might not have happened. Surely the ice storm would have chosen a different route or just died out altogether. Tension returned, confidence fled.

Danielle resumed her death grip on the steering wheel and concentrated now on the road ahead.

The sky which had been overcast, had grown more opaque. It was now a uniform gray, the gray of deck paint, old barns and stormy sea paintings. The light behind it was a presence; she felt excited by that light. It was the same light she had watched many times with her father in the backyard when the poplars whipped and the cottonwoods turned their leaves over. It was storm light and she steeled herself for what she knew was coming. She wasn't in her safe backyard with her strong father this time, though. Now it came. First a few drops on the windshield, then torrents roaring down. She drove slowly with her lights on. The road unwound a few feet at a time. She crawled forward encased in her Toyota, her oriental blue metal submarine. Her throat closed up, as it did now whenever she anticipated that oblivion might be near. She reasoned it would stop soon. It couldn't rain that hard for long. It eventually did lessen in intensity and settle into a steady downpour, keeping pace with her along the highway. When she reached Knoxville, Tennessee she left the highway and pulled into the first motel she saw.

It was a truck stop, a large semicircle of one-story units facing a concrete parking lot. The office was in the restaurant at the right edge of the semicircle as she drove in. She had not talked to a soul in two days except the motel clerk in Virginia, the waitress there and a few gas station attendants. She felt estranged from this real world. In the daylight it seemed less tangible to her than the thoughts in which she had been immersed. She got a room, signed for it, paid for it and ordered a carton of milk (for the Instant Breakfast.) She looked around surreptitiously without appearing to look. Nothing registered though. She was too self-conscious to be a good observer. She couldn't describe one person in the place. When her milk came she paid for it and left. She had to come back for her car keys. She had left them on the counter. "I forgot my keys," she said. She had never felt this alone, this exposed. Danger was everywhere. She was afraid to die. She wanted to get it over with once and for all, end all the suspense. She wanted to live forever. She felt like a little girl, not competent at all. Tennessee was an exotic land. She was not connected there, had no support systems.

When she got to her room it seemed a haven, although not a very attractive one. She took from the car only the things she needed for the night. Her phone rang. It was a man's voice. He saw her in the restaurant, he was a truck driver, he was lonely, wasn't she lonely too. He asked her to have dinner with him. She explained that she did not meet strange men for dinner, that she really didn't mind being alone and that she wanted to relax. He persisted; maybe they could just have a cup of coffee. She was curious she had to admit it, she was also a little flattered. She could not have met him for coffee in a million years. He was a headline **Trucker Kills Syracuse Woman at Tennessee Truck Stop**. She worried that he would knock on her door later, he must know her room number if he had called her room. She wondered what she would do, or say.

She called her mother. "Mom, I can't go any farther. There's a terrible ice storm from Memphis to the middle of Texas." Her mother didn't know what to do. She couldn't save Danielle this time. She was too far away.

In the morning Danielle called all the car dealers in Knoxville. What kind of deal could they give her on her Toyota? Could they take it off her hands? It was too new, she owed too much money, she would never get enough for it. She drew deep breaths, sighed, pulled herself up straight and prepared herself to get back on the road.

When she checked out she tried to figure out which of the men in the restaurant had called her room last night. She couldn't really stare at them and so she gave up. She would never know. It was odd to look at a room full of men believing that one of them recognized her. She got out of there.

The road from Knoxville, Tennessee to Nashville was gorgeous and treacherous. The sky was overcast again but it wasn't raining. The storm warnings were still out. Memphis was getting closer.

The road was cut along a sheer cliff of shale. She rode on the side hugging the shale wall. The other side of the road was hugged by the void. It ran along the edge of another sheer cliff face, but this one descended. She was lucky she was on the ascending side, even though there were fallen rock zones every few miles. She could not have driven on the other side. With the security of the deep gray stone beside her she could occasionally look out over the void to the green land beyond, although with no sun to warm the colors they did not stand out.

She climbed slowly, the Toyota reluctant to make the climb. It was not a car built for travel, it was a car built for transportation. The engine whined a little all the way. She grew more tense as she climbed, her ears filled with pressure. She gulped and yawned trying to equalize it. Although esthetically she appreciated her surroundings she had technically quit driving in Knoxville. She had no desire to drive all the way to Tucson by herself now. She was looking for a way out.

At the top of the climb was a little mountain town called Rockland. Danielle fell in love with it. She thought she might want to live there some day. She didn't know why she loved it. It wasn't a beautiful town, at least not the part near the highway. But it looked small and safe, as if everyone knew everyone and had to tolerate each other's differences because they were stuck with each other. She got gas there and bought a soda, looking over her triptik as she drank it. Nashville was not far but she had to go down the other side of this natural wonder to get to it. She sighed again, gathered her belongings and got back into the blue metal torture chamber.

· · · · ·

At least she knew where her fear of heights came from. It was her last year in college. She had brought a car back to school with her. It was a fifty-dollar special, an old red Dodge boat of a car with black on the sides and red and black fins sticking out aquatically in the rear. She couldn't drive it when she bought it, she didn't have a license but her roommates, Jackie and Alicia, were both from Long Island. They learned to drive in the cauldron of do or die. They forced Danielle to drive the car. They forced her to take her test for the second time. And after she got her license they made her keep driving.

They decided that she would go home with Jackie to Long Island on semester break. Spring was coming but there was still snow on the sides of the roads. They took turns driving and somewhere near Newburgh they stopped at a service area for coffee. They had just reentered the Thruway and they were accelerating. Suddenly they all, at the same moment, noticed the back doors of a tractor-trailer immediately in front of them. They had not seen any taillights or reflectors. The tractor-trailer was decelerating on the hill. A car was passing on the left so Jackie, thinking quickly pulled out on the right shoulder. It would have been fine if it wasn't a double tractor-trailer and if it wasn't for the ice. Suddenly they were airborne, the big old Dodge carving a clumsy slow-motion ballet through the darkness. They landed in a gorge, probably would have flipped over, but the rear of the Dodge caught on a huge old tree stump and glided slowly to a stop in a stand of slender white birches. They just looked at each other, they knew they were lucky to be alive.

As they were getting out of the car two men arrived. One man said that he was a priest, he had thought they were dead, he had all the sacraments with him for extreme unction. Extreme unction to a Lutheran, a Methodist and a Jewess. They started to giggle in a hysterical, breathless chitter.

25

Shock had set in. Alicia had hit her head on the windshield. Other than that they were uninjured.

The priest and his companion said that they would give the girls a ride to the next service area so that they could report the accident. They were afraid that no one would know the car was down there. They had seen it go off the road but otherwise it was not visible from the highway.

When they reported to the State Police at the next service area the police were very angry with them. They should have stayed with the car the police said. By now Danielle, Jackie and Alicia were crying steadily. They couldn't stop shaking. The police put the three of them in the back of the police car. They drove them back the way they had come at ninety miles an hour, the three women wailing all the way. They suddenly whipped over to the shoulder of the road right on a high bridge. The three sobbed louder and cringed with fear. They made Danielle and her two roommates watch the radar while they clocked a speeder. They were sure the girls had been speeding. They didn't believe the tractor-trailer with no rear reflectors or lights.

When the policemen felt the three had been suitably chastened they drove to the state police station at the next exit. They probably didn't mean to be unjust. Perhaps they were imagining their own daughters in a similar situation. But the injustice of their implications added more shudders to the symphony of sobs. Alicia called her father who agreed to come get them in the morning. They called a college friend in Newburgh and went to his house to spend the night. His mother cosseted them and fed them hot chocolate. They watched the Glenn Miller story and had a good excuse to cry some more.

Danielle remembers seeing the poor old totaled Dodge when they towed it to the police station. The car had a face, and that face had a humorous, sad expression. Both headlights were hanging askew looking like popped eyeballs;

the broken grill looked like a broken nose and the front bumper hung down in a perfect parody of clownish grief.

●   ●   ●   ●   ●

That had all happened when she didn't believe in death. Now she did. She rocketed down the back side of the cliff road in her blue metal guided missile pointed straight at Nashville. Actually she limped into Nashville as if the new Toyota was that old, sad, red Dodge. She was turning in her keys, hanging up her registration. She picked a Howard Johnson's to stay in this time. She felt the need of a little luxury. Shake the truck stop blues. It was a nice room. It had sliding glass doors. She could park her car right outside. It wasn't raining in Nashville either but the weather report was the same; the ice storm was out there.

She thumbed through the yellow pages while she sipped her Instant Breakfast: Auto Rental, Auto Repair, Auto Sales and Service. Somewhere in there Danielle saw a listing for Auto Drive-Away. God is good, she thought as she dialed the number. The business was run by a young college student. He would pick up the car in the morning and he would be glad to drop her off at the bus station. He'd get her car to Tucson as soon as possible. The deal was set.

Danielle hauled everything in out of the trunk and the backseat. She separated what she would take with her from what she would ship on the bus. She packed the things for shipping and labeled them. She put them back in the car. Then she soaked in a hot tub.

She never believed people who said that Nashville had a beat; that the whole city swam to the twang of country guitars. But that's the sound that eased her down to sleep in the strange motel bed. Her first hint of the West.

In the morning she signed the paper leaving her little baby Toyota to strangers. It cost her three hundred fifty of her precious dollars. She brought her bus ticket, another

27

sixty-three dollars, paid for shipping her bundles, ninety-three dollars. Being spineless was expensive. The college student wasn't sure when her car would get to Tucson, not until the weather broke probably.

She sighed again, this time with relief and sank back into the bus seat. She left the driving to them. There was no ice in Memphis, the roads were dry. They crossed the Mississippi. They were in Arkansas.

4
Arkansas and Texas

In Arkansas, safely ensconced in her velour bus seat, Danielle rode through a glass tunnel, the aftermath of the storm. The roads were clear but everything else was dripping with glistening crystal jewelry. This small part of the wide world was transformed in silent icy, ethereal majesty. Danielle thought about people who had been caught on that same highway while it was happening. How could they have survived? She was amazed that there were not piles of cars on the divides. Maybe people had given in and waited out the storm but she had seen people who would drive at normal speeds through the deepest blizzard, the most blinding rain. Maybe there really were Supermen (and women) with X-ray vision and nerves of steel. Maybe thinking you were invulnerable made you so, and, of course, vice versa. So, although every twig and every blade of grass glowed inside its icy coat to create a world of brittle lace, unreal, fragile and evanescent; even beauty had to share space with risk. Danielle shivered.

By the time they rode into Little Rock the crystalline wardrobe had been put away in the closet, the bare brown branches of winter had been revealed. It was bitter cold. Danielle read her book, she did crossword puzzles, she dozed, she occasionally glanced out the window. It was heavenly. Through the night the bus went wherever the bus driver pointed it. He was fearless, he was a machine. She trusted him implicitly. When morning came they were in Texas.

Danielle didn't know what she expected of Texas but it was the loneliest place she had ever seen. They stopped at a little diner in the middle of nowhere. A biting, whining wind tore at them, they being the only obstacles in its path. It was perfectly flat land with nothing visible anywhere around the little diner. Later, once again in motion, they passed land with scrubby bushes dotted here and there, rail fences, oil wells in almost every field. Danielle thought of the word chaparral from TV cowboy movies. She didn't know if this was it but she redefined it if it wasn't. She saw cattle dead by the side of the road, huddled under low bushes, covered with frost. Someone got off at a crossroads. The bus driver just left him there with his suitcases. A long road, empty of any signs of life, vanished as a tiny dot into some distant brown hills. Where was this person going? Why wasn't someone already there waiting to pick him up? She worried that he would end up like the frosty cows. "Whatever you do, don't lie down," she thought.

They were driving into Dallas. The glass and steel buildings looked frozen too. There were no people on the streets. They pulled into the Greyhound terminal but they didn't stay long. They changed drivers and hit the road again. Westward ho. Danielle tried to sleep. She couldn't. Her mind drifted to the time in her life just before she left for Tucson.

• • • • •

Audrey Ann and Nicole had already left Syracuse. She and her sister Lily took a flat together on the east side of the city. Lily was about five years younger than Danielle. She was born after Danielle's brother. Lily was a secretary at a law office. She was the tallest girl in the family with a pretty face and long dark blonde hair. She was a bit of a spoiled brat at this point, possibly because she was the baby, possibly it was just that she had lived at home up to now and didn't have the experience to sympathize with the concerns of others.

The flat they rented was fancy, a huge living room with wall to wall carpeting and a brick fireplace at one end with high windows on each side. The mantle was layered inward in several stages and painted the same off white as the walls. There was a tiny screened-in front porch off the living room. The carpeting continued into the dining room and there was a crystal chandelier in the center of the room. The kitchen was old-fashioned with high white cupboards and a breakfast nook. There were also three bedrooms and a bath. The back bedroom had a screened-in porch attached but the room was really too cold to use. All the bedrooms had hardwood floors.

Not only was the apartment beautiful but the landlord who lived upstairs was also beautiful. He wasn't a tall guy, maybe 5' 8". He didn't have a beautiful body, he had a tendency towards a slight belly and she was sure he had love handles. But he had a handsome, intelligent, expressive face with thick dark brown hair, a full beard and a mustache. He had deep brown eyes and they crinkled at the corners. She tried to imagine his face without the beard and mustache but she couldn't. His name was Michael Berger, he was a stock broker, a great cook and he had an eye for color and design.

Michael practically lived at Danielle's flat after work. He cooked meals with Danielle and Lily; they all watched TV together every night until after the 11:00 news while Danielle graded papers. But it was a totally platonic relationship, after the news he would always climb the stairs to his own apartment.

Although Danielle found him interesting, Lily did not care for him much. She didn't have a real problem with his hanging around, although the two of them fought a lot. They fought about mushrooms, about television shows, about Scrabble words. Lily would often end up pouting in a corner of a couch somewhere. Michael would still have the same tender, understanding smile on his face. Danielle could see how it might be a bit maddening. Actually for all Lily's lack of experience she was closer to the truth than Danielle was on this one.

Lily tried to warn Danielle about him, she thought he collected broken hearts for ego strokes; that Danielle was falling in love, but he was not. When Nicole came into Syracuse to take care of some business, she met Michael and took an instant dislike to him. Danielle decided he probably was a schmuck if Nicole thought so, Nicole had good judgment in these matters, but, after all nothing was going on, so all the warning seemed inappropriate. Except, she was, of course, already more involved than she realized.

Several of Michael's ex-girlfriends came to visit. Danielle met them. There seemed to be some bitterness on their part about the way Michael had treated them but they were willing to give him another try. Each time they went home empty-handed (actually, empty-ring-fingered) and were never heard from again.

He went to a conference. He met a "gorgeous beauty" from an old Texas oil family. Now every night when he came downstairs he left early to call her long distance. He wanted to marry her, he proposed over and over again. She was twice divorced. She wanted to take her time.

Danielle listened. She tried to analyze the relationship with him, as she used to do with Audrey Ann, Amanda and Nicole. But in her secret mind she didn't believe he would ever marry the oily heiress. She never consciously expressed it even to herself, but of course she thought that some day he would see the jewel he had right downstairs in his own house.

It was Fall; he came to Thanksgiving dinner at the downstairs flat. Danielle's whole family was there. Danielle and Lily had to rent tables. For the first time Danielle was a little embarrassed by her family. They seemed so provincial and simple. Who were these people? She felt guilty of betrayal. And she loved them very much, although, at the moment in a sort of condescending way. Now they seemed the sheltered children and she the worldly adult. She was seeing her family through Michael's eyes. No oil millionaires here.

Danielle gave a Christmas party. She invited her colleagues from the college. She cooked for days. There was a buffet set up in the dining room, with home-baked sliced turkey and ham. There were home-baked rolls, sweet and sour kielbasa, a relish tray, and a huge chef salad each ingredient in a separate dish so that people could put it together themselves. There were sixteen varieties of home-baked Christmas cookies including cut outs frosted as works of art, gingerbread men and those Scottish tea balls that bulge with pecans and are rolled in powdered sugar. She had a fire burning in the fireplace, a huge Christmas tree glittering in the corner. She had bought all kinds of liquor, wines and beers. But the piéce de resistance was the eggnog made with medium cream and cognac. Lily helped her do it all, but she was doubtful. She felt Danielle hopes for the evening would be frustrated.

Sometimes that Lily was a really smart girl. It was a good party. It lasted late and got rowdy with eating and drinking, dancing and flirting. She was a bit embarrassed when Michael showed up in summer white pants and an outdated, loud, multicolored shirt with some outlandish footwear -- what were they? -- sandals! Danielle refused to be superficial. Her kamikaze crush would not be so easily quashed. Michael talked to all the guests, the female guests in particular. He believed he had great charm with women. He never got drunk. Danielle didn't know what she had expected. But Lily was correct, it didn't happen.

Danielle had met Michael's two children from his previous marriage. They were great kids, Joshua was eight, Esther was five, both with their father's dark hair and eyes. They often wandered through Danielle's flat on the weekends they spent with their father. They accepted her as a neighbor, but they were not terribly interested in her. Danielle comforted Michael when his first wife remarried. He began to mention his own marriage more often.

He decided to go to Texas. He would take the kids with him. Who could resist those sweet faces? He would come home engaged at the very least. There was a major blizzard in Syracuse while he was gone. Danielle was 5 feet, 2 inches tall; the snow banks were over her head. People tied red plastic streamers on their car radio antennas so they wouldn't hit each other at intersections. Every corner was a blind one. Danielle and Lily shoveled until they couldn't lift any more snow. The banks were too high. Then they called one of the many people who attached plows to their trucks every winter to do driveways. Their guy was inexperienced or indifferent. He should have plowed the snow out of the driveway, but he plowed it in, towards the garage. There was so much of it and it was so heavy that he couldn't get it past the back door. It rained the next day and coated all the snowbanks with ice. The snow was there until Spring. Where was your landlord when you needed him? Danielle felt Michael left on purpose right then because he knew it was going to snow. She started thinking then about sunny places. She started to see the writing on the wall, to make contingency plans.

Michael and the kids returned at four o'clock in the morning. Danielle had been worried about them, she had waited up. He brought the sleepy, blinking children in through Danielle's house. He was carrying Esther wrapped in a blanket. Joshua had pink creased cheeks and was walking with a waver. Michael put a hand on his shoulder to steady him. He said that he didn't know how he got home, he didn't remember long stretches of the road. He thought he was driving in his sleep. Danielle was appalled that he could risk his children like that. But he was usually an excellent father. He took the sleepy children upstairs. Danielle went to bed. She was a hard case.

They took the children out to breakfast at the All Night Egg Plant. They read the Sunday **New York Times**. The restaurant had hired a string quartet. They felt like they were in New York. They lingered. To Danielle it proved how good they were together. They were magic. She felt personally responsible for the string quartet. He didn't say anything about Texas, he didn't say if he was an engaged man or not.

• • • • •

On the Greyhound, Danielle finally dozed. When she woke up they were two hours from El Paso. She tried to do a crossword puzzle but it didn't hold her interest. She returned to her thoughts. She didn't want to remember this part but she had ended on a minor chord and completion was required.

• • • • •

Finally Danielle got frustrated with the whole platonic mess. She demanded to know "what am I, chopped liver?" "Why aren't you interested in me? I'm right here, alive, in the flesh. Do you only love women who are far away?"

He confessed that he liked her, he even said she was prettier than his woman in Texas. He was confused. He took her to bed. It wasn't a disaster, but it wasn't great. Danielle knew he wasn't for her, but she couldn't let go.

He still came by every night. Her feelings were in turmoil. Finally, one night, after Michael had gone up to bed, Danielle followed him upstairs. She said she needed to be comforted. He was her best friend now that Audrey Ann and Nicole were gone. He took her into his bed. Natural urges took their course. But it didn't change anything, it was sad, it was good bye.

This is when Danielle finally learned that she was not immortal; this is when she understood the message of her sister's death and her aunt's suicide. We are very fragile, there is no one protecting us, we are all alone and the end could come at any moment. This was when she began to picture herself in sunny hammocks with sliced wrists, blood dripping. She didn't feel safe around knives. This is when she stopped being able to swallow. It was no longer an unthinking, involuntary act. Each swallow took conscious thought and effort. Everywhere she went she saw the poster on choking. She took it as an omen. She moved home with her parents and went into therapy. By the time she left for Tucson she weighed 107 pounds. She looked great. She didn't know it. One part of her mind was waging war on her will to survive and take her chances in the games.

* * * * *

Remembering all this was exhausting. Danielle felt tired now, very tired. She slept. When she woke up the bus was pulling into El Paso.

The bus stopped in El Paso for a couple of hours. Danielle felt grimy; she had been wearing the same clothes for over two days. She hadn't been able to do more than splash cold water on her face. She went to the ladies room. Bus stations are what they are everywhere, generally dreary and littered. No one looks chic in a bus station, and Danielle believed she was even a bit too frowzy for this company. She scrubbed her face with the washcloth from her shoulder bag. She brushed her teeth. She washed her hair in the sink and wrapped it in the towel she had with her. Other patrons of the ladies room avoided the sink where she stood. They thought she was one of those ladies who had taken up residence at the bus station. She turned up the air flow tube on the sanitary hand dryer and pushed the button again and again until her hair was dry. Then she paid ten cents for privacy and changed her clothes. Gradually she began to feel less gritty, more alert, more confident. She left the ladies room a new person.

Danielle stood in line at the ticket counter to ask what time she would get into Tucson. Four a.m. they said. She started to worry about where she would stay when she got there. Without a car she needed to be near the college. She looked over her Chamber of Commerce street map of Tucson. She decided to stay at the YWCA. In New York City she had stayed at a YWCA; it was clean and cheap. She called the one in Tucson and explained that she wouldn't arrive until four in the morning. They said they would tell the night watchman to keep an eye out for her. "Thank you, see you later." She hung up and bought a soda. It was time to board the bus.

There were several friendly people on the bus this time. They were sitting near Danielle, two guys and a girl in their early twenties. Before long they were talking with Danielle, they wanted to know where she was going and why. She answered their questions. They looked a little wild, fringed jackets, too much hair, tattoos, ragged dirty jeans; but after all the speechless days Danielle welcomed the company. They played cards and talked all the way to Tucson. They were headed for San Diego. That suited Danielle just fine. At Tucson she waved good bye and left the bus. She was finally here; the only person in the modern world who ever took six days and spent over six hundred dollars getting here. Canastoga wagons were probably faster, certainly cheaper. While not exactly the triumphant entry of a modern, self-sufficient woman; enter Tucson she did, right out through the grimy double doors of the bus station

5
Tucson

There were taxis outside the door of the bus station but Danielle's bundles had not yet arrived. They were a couple of days behind her. She got in a cab.

"Where to," the cab driver said.

"The YWCA," she said.

So far Danielle might as well not have left New York. The cab driver gave a sour look and started out. Still familiar territory. She paid the cab driver and knocked on the door of the Y. The night watchman turned out to be a young college-age man with an open, friendly way about him. He made Danielle feel better than she had in days.

"I've done some traveling myself," he sympathized. "You can't get a bed right now. It's too late, it would disturb everybody, but I'll show you where the shower room is. You can take a shower and sleep on a couch in the lounge until everyone gets up."

That sounded great to Danielle. They climbed a staircase behind the front desk to the upstairs lounge. It was a large, surprisingly pleasant room open to the staircase on one side, except for a railing. The couch looked comfortable but Danielle wasn't sleepy. She wanted to be clean. She took over the shower room; it was large with several shower stalls just like the ones in the dorm at college, and a half dozen sinks, several toilet stalls, but she was the only one there. She could wander at will. She groomed herself at a leisurely pace, luxuriating in the spaciousness of the room and the quiet of the early morning hours. She packed everything back in the appropriate bag and moved out to the lounge. It was dark and comforting. She even smoked a cigarette; thoughts empty for the moment, just enjoying the peace. Then she went to sleep.

It was a rude awakening. The other tenants of the Y got up early. Danielle was in shock. It was 7:30 a.m. As soon as she saw her "roommates" Danielle knew she couldn't stay here and hold on to her sanity. These women did not have a firm hold on reality. They had lost their grip. Danielle, on the edge of slipping herself, did not want to be pushed.

Her first clue was when the director arrived. She had none of the charm of the night watchman.

"Why are you sleeping on the couch?"

She was the kind of woman you called ma'am. Danielle explained how she came to be there.

"Come with me."

She led Danielle to a bed in a large dormitory room. Her bed was in the middle portion of the room against a wall. There were laundry-clean sheets and towels in a pile on one end of the bed. She also had a locker. There were about fifteen or twenty beds in the room. On the bed next to hers was a woman curled in the fetal position talking to herself. All of the other women were beginning to move about. Her "neighbor" did not look ready to rise and shine. Neither did the others for that matter. They moved sullenly for the most part, their eyes were dim or overly bright, their faces guarded or out of control. They were her second clue. Danielle's impulse was to grab her things and get out of there. She imagined that this was twilight zone stuff, you wandered in, unsuspecting, and never emerged again.

Her third, and by now unnecessary, clue was when she walked to the tiny kitchenette to make herself a cup of coffee. There was a jar of Maxwell House instant available for general use. Deposit a dime in the cup. She was putting the teakettle on when another woman walked in, a "normal" looking woman.

"Would you like a cup of coffee," Danielle asked carefully.

"Don't talk to me, " answered the cheerful morning companion. She began shaking and wringing her hands. She muttered something about lizards and hair.

Danielle wasn't sure how to jump into that conversation. She took her coffee out into the lounge and drank it very fast. She rushed back into the kitchenette and washed her cup. She grabbed her pocketbook and her map and she was out of there. She vowed to herself that she would find an apartment before the sun set. Usually she would only feel sympathy for these troubled women, but she had had very little sleep, she was alone in a strange city and her own grip on sanity was precarious. Perhaps insuring self-survival through humor is a very deep and unconscious impulse.

According to her map the "Y" was around the corner and several blocks south of the University. She decided that she wanted to at least set foot on the campus. She turned the corner and walked north. What she saw did not immediately enchant her. The light from the sun was too bright. She thought perhaps Salvador Dali had formed a partnership with God in one of Salvador's previous incarnations or when he was just part of the general atom pool, and talked God into using these stark fluorescent lights over Tucson just to mess with peoples' minds.

Also, although she had known ahead of time that this was the desert, she had not expected it to be so, well, dusty. Nothing was really green; everything looked like a silvery-green relative of dusty miller. She expected the desert to be beautiful. Danielle began to think that she had made a terrible mistake leaving her lush green home for this. She temporarily forgot that Syracuse was, at the moment, probably knee deep in snow.

She began to suspect that it would be all right when she passed the little pink stucco house, set up on a slight rise, postage stamp front yard filled with at least twenty different Christmas trees, each one decorated with its own theme - one with bird seed balls and suet, one with ribbon curled and

41

hanging, one with tiny chimes tinkling softly, and so on. That was the spirit of Tucson as she had imagined it. It somehow made her lighter and more carefree. It had humor. She thought she heard Audrey Ann chortle.

The college was about five blocks from the little pink house. You walked straight on to the campus at the end of the street. The campus had green grass. It was groomed and landscaped. There were trees. The first building she saw was a big old wood and brick structure with a veranda around it and a tower at the top. There was a phone booth, one of the outdoor kind with just a short plastic rectangular box built on a pole to contain the phone, looking rather out-of-place in the middle of the green lawn in front of the building.

Danielle called home. "Hi Mom, I'm here." "Yes, finally." "I'm standing right on the front lawn at the college." She told her mother about the car and the Y. Her mother told her how relieved they all were that she got there safely. Danielle said she'd keep in touch. "I love you, Mom. Good bye." Her family was very far away. She wanted to keep her mother on the phone, keep her talking, but she knew her mother got nervous spending money on long distance. It was a generational thing.

The bookstore was open so Danielle took a quick tour of it. The cafeteria was next door to the bookstore, it had tables outside as well as inside, it had a wall of windows on either side of the doors. She bought a bowl of corn chowder and a roll. Very few people were there. School wouldn't start for another two weeks.

Reluctantly she left the campus. She was wasting time. She had to find an apartment, today. She was not sleeping at the Y.

Danielle didn't have her car; she didn't know where to start looking. Tucson is a widespread city. It has residential neighborhoods in all directions. Houses mingle with businesses in most areas. You can travel forty miles in Tucson in a single day, just doing errands. Luckily Danielle didn't know this yet. Then she really would have been overwhelmed. She walked south away from the college; her basic plan to get a newspaper and look at what was available. There were several corner groceries between the college and the Y. Danielle stopped and got a newspaper. She passed a two-story apartment house that wrapped itself around a corner. It had a "for rent" sign. Within fifteen minutes she had an apartment. She returned gleefully to the Y, picked up her meager belongings, thanked her lucky stars and moved into the corner basement apartment.

It was not lovely, but it was home. She immediately moved the furniture just to show it who was boss. It was a damp, one-room place with a kitchen at one end, bath off the kitchen and a living room that also served as the bedroom. It was furnished with a few tables, a mattress and box springs on the floor. Outside her door was a courtyard with a minute swimming tank (heated, the sign said) and a concrete patio inside a chain link fence. The complex was full of birdlike Arab women and children, so thin they seemed to have hollow bones, who twittered at each other in their native language. The women wore skirts at all times and, although they did not have to cover their faces, they had to keep their hair covered. The children, not yet subject to the rules for adults, although the little girls also wore dresses, played in the dirt around the edges of the patio or followed their mothers in their daily chores. Sayed, the manager who rented Danielle the apartment left some religious literature with her. He was a young handsome man in western dress who obviously enjoyed his patriarchal position in the compound.

Danielle still had no one to talk to. She had gone from the loonies to the loons. She set about feathering her nest, which is difficult to do with only the contents of one large shoulder bag and an army knapsack. Her clothes were unwearable. They looked like an eagle would turn them down as nest material. Her iron was in a bus somewhere in

Texas. She needed an iron and an ironing board. Danielle consulted her street map.

She got the iron and ironing board at J.C. Penney downtown. It hadn't been easy. She started to wonder when her car would get here. Now, at least, she had something to do. She could iron clothes.

There was a motel down the street with a restaurant. She had breakfast there the next morning. She called the bus station. "Are my packages there yet?" After two days they were. Danielle took a cab and moved her possessions from the bus station to the apartment. This cab driver was not happy, but she was thrilled to have all her things around her again.

Danielle brought a lot of nonessentials with her. She brought two oil paintings by a Syracuse painter. He was an art teacher at the college who used to hold sales of his work each year for colleagues until his work became too expensive for a professor's meager resources. She had a set of pottery water glasses, a pottery carafe with wine cups, whimsical pottery Irish coffee mugs, and a pottery teapot all made by her old college roommate, Jackie, who was now a potter. She lingered over each item as she lifted it out of the packing. She was beginning to feel whole again. There was her iron (old anyway), her radio, her TV. She decorated the dungeon, sat down, checked it out, moved things around.

She was still lonely though. She walked around among her things talking to herself. Loneliness could make you strange; it could drive you crazy. If school didn't start soon she would end up back at the YWCA, permanently. She rented a car for a couple of days and poked around Tucson. She almost got in an accident. She was so busy looking at mountains. She found a shopping mall. One more step on the road to mental health.

Danielle was spending too much money. She stopped renting the car. She only went to places she could walk to. Danielle's status symbols were dropping off like feathers during molting.   The assistant professor title went, the teaching was gone, the colleagues shed, the friends fled, the family left behind, the couches, chairs, tables, bed all temporarily plucked away; without the car she felt naked. She wanted to hide and wait for her new plumage to grow in but the apartment and the lack of company drove her out. That's where the new feathers were anyway.

Sundays were the worst. Sunday is a long, long day when you don't need it to catch up on your laundry or your paperwork, when there are no social engagements on your calendar. Danielle didn't go to church anymore. She didn't think God had calling hours, she didn't believe he scheduled "at homes." She called Southwestern Bell and got a phone. But even a call home didn't fill up a whole lot of Sunday.

She waited. She waited for her car to come, she waited for school to start, she waited for her life to start up again. It's a pity we never know what's coming. Obviously some force in the universe felt that extraordinary events were called for at this juncture in Danielle's life. If Danielle had known, she might have enjoyed her solitude more.

6
Tucson

Danielle got in the line outside the building where the students registered for classes. It was a long line that curled around the building, across the parking lot and on to the green lawn. Now she knew she was back at college. There were no special lines for people who had been assistant professors for nine years. Everyone was the same; everyone was just a student. The line moved quickly, actually she was inside the building before she had a chance to plan how she would proceed, a chance to remember the process.

It was a large room with tables around the edges, A-E, F-M, N-Z, with other tables labeled "Wildcats" and "transfer students", "graduate students" and a few cages in the center each labeled "cashier". There were ropes leading to each area to keep people in line, like Disney World.

Danielle stood uncertainly in the center of the floor. She was trying to get her bearings. She didn't know where to start. She saw a young woman headed towards her. She realized she was about to be rescued. This was by far the friendliest looking contemporary she had seen since Audrey Ann and Nicole. Her name was Kate, Katherine, and she was from New York. She grew up in a small town outside of New York City, called New Paltz. Her father had been a professor at the State University. A lot of people in Tucson are from New York. In fact, a lot of people in Tucson are not from Tucson. Meeting someone who has lived in Tucson long enough to be considered a native is rare. They probably are kept in sanctuaries as an endangered species.

Kate Grandy was grand. She took Danielle with her through the registration process, saw to it that she got the classes she wanted or needed, stayed with her right to the paying. When she realized Danielle was walking home, she offered a ride. She took Danielle's phone number. It was a beginning.

Classes still didn't start for a week, so for a few days Danielle's life fell back into the lonely pattern that it had previously followed.

Kate called, "Hi Danielle, would you like to go shopping." Danielle didn't know how she could fit that into her busy schedule, actually she didn't want to seem overly eager. She said in her most unneedy voice, "Yes, that sounds nice."

Kate said she would be right over. They went to the El Con mall on Broadway, the big one. Kate was a careful shopper; she didn't go to buy out the shops. Danielle could see that she was very practical, that her needs were simple. Danielle decided not to let Kate see what a spendthrift she was, at least not right away. Danielle was nervous, she really wanted Kate for a friend.

"What are you studying?" Danielle asked Kate as they walked along. Actually Kate was a speed walker with long legs. She walked. Danielle half ran to keep up. Danielle was used to that. That was the way she and her sister Laura used to walk to church. Danielle's spiked heels had left deep craters in the hot tar roads. Now, thank goodness, flat shoes were in style. She left no marks.

"I'm studying social work," Kate said. "Working part time and going to school part time. I need about eight more courses for my master's."

"Where do you work?"

"Department of Social Services, Division for Youth," Kate told her.

They went to a fabric shop. Kate wanted to make a pillow for her couch. They had pillows already stamped out on calico with designs on the front, kittens, little girls holding hands. Danielle could sew also, but she didn't have her machine (actually her mother's) with her.

"You can use mine if you decide you want to make something," Kate said.

Danielle was surprised that Kate was so open and friendly. Danielle was surprised how guarded she had become. She already knew, however, that she trusted Kate. Danielle generally saw women much more clearly than she saw men. She was glad that Kate seemed to take friendship for granted. When Kate dropped Danielle off at home they were still talking.

"One of the things I really miss is good music," Danielle mentioned. "I couldn't bring my stereo and my radio is awful."

"I have a stereo tape deck you can borrow," Kate told her. "I'll bring it over next time I come."

Again Danielle was amazed that this woman would trust an acquaintance with her stereo. The new Danielle could not have been so generous. She didn't dare mention anything else she needed. Danielle was not a taker. She usually provided herself with what she needed or did without. She knew that she could be trusted not to rip Kate off, so she allowed herself to accept Kate's generosity.

Sunday was still a bad day, but this Sunday Danielle entertained herself by picking out twelve tapes and one for the gold box from the Columbia House music club ad. She sent it in. You only had to pay one dollar. Classes started on Wednesday so Danielle went through her clothes and picked out something to wear, ironed it and hung it carefully away from the other clothes in the closet.

She was beginning to hate this apartment. While she was sitting on the couch, á la bed, á la mattress on the floor, a cricket suddenly jumped across the spread. Danielle jumped higher than the cricket. She moved the furniture. She wanted the mattress on the inside wall, instead of the outside wall. She had one nice chair, a walnut and black canvas sling chair that she had bought at Penney's. However, her charging days were almost over.

49

First class -- Danielle felt the way she had every year on the first day since her school career began. Even as a teacher she had felt this exciting anxiety. But now she was stripped of her title, her collegiality. She was fifteen again, it was the first day of high school, except she was also thirty-two, a veteran teacher; odd sensation. Her first class was on the third floor, she stood in the back of the elevator waiting for the sliding doors to close, talking out loud to herself. Just as the doors were about to close, almost safe from discovery, a handsome young man walked in the front doors, looked right at her, caught her in the act. She blushed, he laughed. When Danielle walked through the open door of her first classroom she found that he was her first professor. How embarrassing. She couldn't look at him. She had to, the seats were arranged in a square, seminar style. They had to introduce themselves and tell why they were there. When it was her turn to speak he said, "Yes, haven't we already met somewhere?" with what she assessed as a devilish smirk. College looks interesting, she thought, as she introduced herself. Now though, she didn't dare say she came for the sunshine. She mumbled something about the school's reputation, the faculty.

He was an excellent, married professor (she noted the ring). He didn't assign a text; instead he assigned four pages of journal articles to read all related to learning theory. They would discuss issues, not facts. Danielle was hooked; she remembered how much she loved learning. A classmate, Mary offered her a ride home. Danielle took it. Perhaps she had found another friend.

Mary Abbott was a nervous girl; she talked fast with a catch in her voice. But Danielle liked her immediately. She was interesting and intelligent. Mary was also from New York but she had come to Tucson to meet some friends who were already living there. When they got to Danielle's place Mary didn't come in. Danielle said goodbye in the parking lot, took her school books and headed for the dungeon.

The next day Auto Drive-Away called and said her car had arrived. Danielle couldn't wait to see the little blue metal desert wanderer. She took a cab to South Tucson and picked it up. You couldn't even tell anyone had been in it. As soon as she got behind the wheel she felt one little piece of her personal power falling back in place. She knew things are not power, but she couldn't help it. She had wheels. She took a cruise down Speedway Blvd.

Her second class was an evening class, rather less inspiring than the first. She had her parking sticker now so she drove herself home. It was semi-dark when she arrived back at the cellar. She heard happy chattering and quiet laughter coming from the pool area. It was a cold night, but as she looked through the protective shrubbery she saw that the pool was lit. Steam rose off the water and dissipated in the cool dry desert night. One of the young Arab mothers and a child, probably her daughter, were diving and surfacing like baby porpoises at play. It looked so inviting, but obviously so private a moment. Danielle continued into her gloomy cricket den (she tried to remember that crickets are good luck in China) and did some reading before she went to bed. When she went out to her car in the morning there was an inch of snow on it and on everything else. She was disgusted and enchanted. She knew it didn't happen often. She thought perhaps, the rear window defroster and snow tires on her blue metal climate hopper had fooled a passing cloud into dumping its load early.

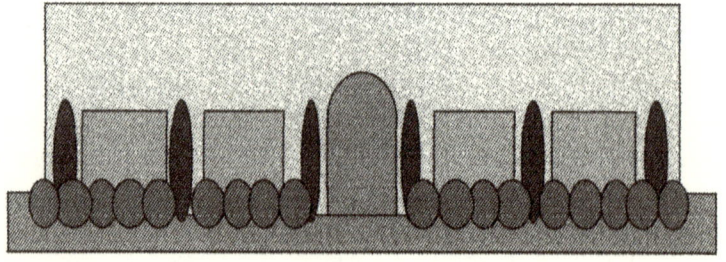

7

Tucson

Kate called.

"Hi Danielle, how would you like to go have breakfast in the desert?

"Really? That sounds great, who's going?"

Danielle couldn't believe it. She hadn't even seen the desert yet. Now she was going with Kate who obviously knew her way around a cactus.

"We're going with my boyfriend Stuart and his friend Carson."

It sounded like a blind date. Danielle started getting nervous. But she had to go; this was what she came here for. This was life. She wanted to forget her fears and her disappointments. Where did this resilience come from? She wanted to see the desert and, of course, now she couldn't wait to see this Carson character.

"Wear jeans," Kate said. "We're going Saturday morning, pick you up at 8:00."

What did you wear on your feet when you went to the desert? Desert boots, of course, ha. Danielle went through her foot gear, the backless, high-heeled 'Candies' were obviously out; the stretch sandals, no good; she would have cactus spines in her toes. She settled for the short Dexter work shoes and socks. Now the top. A sweatshirt with a short-sleeved shirt underneath in case it was hot. Danielle wanted to be dressed like a native, a real desert rat. Saturday was three days away.

They picked her up right at 8:00. There were two pick-up trucks, only two people, three at the most, could fit in each. They were Fords, apparently only a Ford 2x4 would do. Carson's was red with Ford written in big white letters across the tailgate, all caps. Stuart's was a beat up old black truck also signed Ford, same place, same lettering, although portions of his letters had chipped and fallen away. Carson had his dog, Bandit, in the back and his roommate Jim in the front.

Carson Donahue was everything a cowboy ought to be. He wasn't handsome but he wasn't bad to look at. Short and lean and muscular with a small belly (of course, a beer belly), he wore a flannel shirt, none too new, open over a red T-shirt. His jeans wouldn't quite stand alone but they had never had creases and were worn thin in a number of spots. He had dark brown straight hair that fell over his forehead, long in back, curling on his neck, shorter in front. He was darkly tanned like old leather (what else) with crinkles around his eyes (from looking off towards distant horizons in the bright desert sun, obviously) and he had nice brown eyes, small but kindly, squinty cowboy eyes. He had real cowboy boots, a little down at the heel, dusty from striding desert landscapes. He was from New Jersey. His roommate was a tall big blond Swede, very quiet and shy, dressed also in the local male uniform.

Stuart was a tall, slim, handsome guy, also from New Jersey, very clean with a neatly trimmed medium brown mustache and a full head of hair to match. He was a friendly guy although with a dry sarcastic manner. He had a certain charisma. His boots were clean, so were his pants.

Danielle rode with Kate and Stuart. (All that nervousness for nothing.) They named the cactus for her as they rode along. The one that looked like long, bumpy green fingers with protruding needles, ocatilla; the one with hairy fuzz all over, grandfather cactus, relative of the prickly pear; the prickly pear itself, which looked like Mickey Mouse ears outfitted for Devil's Island; the cholla (choy-ah) and teddy bear cholla and; lord over them all, the giant saguaro. This desert didn't look at all as Danielle had pictured it. It was full of life, not just full of sand. Small mosses, tiny bushes, larger brush and the cactus everywhere.

They pulled up at the edge of a watering hole. No roads went here, you had to know this spot by some arcane landmarks that were not apparent to Danielle. They all collected dry twigs as they walked from the trucks to the edge of the water. Stuart built a ring of stones and then piled the kindling inside. The others went back and unloaded the trucks, the beer first. Beer for breakfast? Eggs and bacon without 'Coors", are you hallucinating? Danielle ate the easy things and they were delicious, flavored with the spice of new adventure.

Carson showed Danielle animal signs. These were the little sika deer hoof prints; these were from the jackrabbit. The hole in the top of the saguaro, that was where the elf owl lived. The dog was not just for looks, he was a hunter. Bandit was a good tracker and a pointer but he was getting old. Almost ready to retire.

They set up their beer cans on a log. The guys got out their guns. Carson had a sawed off shotgun. She was shocked. Danielle had never even seen a real gun. Bandit kept pacing behind the beer cans. Finally they got him out of the shooting gallery. The guys lined up and took their shots. Several cans fell. Some of the shots were long and kicked up dust on the other side of the water hole. Carson wanted Danielle to try it. He showed her how to stand, how to sight, how to deal with the recoil. Danielle felt ridiculous holding the shot gun but she really wanted to hit the target. She sighted down the barrel through the two metal sights. She thought she was prepared. She pulled the trigger. The kick sent her shoulder backward in spite of Carson's warnings. The shot did get across the water, but it was long and wide. She saw the dust fountain when it hit. They all went around the water hole to pick up the shell casings. Danielle felt like she had lost her virginity. She felt a little high. She also felt that she had taken a real wishy-washy stand on the gun issue. No one else seemed the least bit disturbed. They packed up and drove back into town. Kate and Stuart dropped Danielle off at the catacombs. She was too excited to stay inside. She took her assignment out to the patio, lazed in the sun and pretended to read.

Sundays were still quiet. Nothing ever happened on Sunday. But now Danielle had work to do so she didn't notice how long the day was. Sometimes she went to the University library to catch up on her reading. She was whittling away at the four-page list of articles that Dr. Alexander had given them to read. It was interesting. Ten years of research had been completed since she left college. She had meant to keep up with the journals. She liked what George Miller had to say about the limitations of short-term memory. And Noam Chomsky about natural language acquisition and the work Ken and Yetta Goodman, Frank Smith and others had done putting the work from the two fields together, a new word coined, psycholinguistics. On Sundays Danielle lived in a world of words and ideas, a simple world that she understood well.

When she went to her Monday morning class Mary Abbott asked her to have lunch. They went to the school cafeteria. Danielle had soup and a roll again, easy to swallow. Mary had a salad. They talked about the articles they were reading. Mary had dark circles under her eyes; she looked more worried than before.

"How late have you been staying up?" Danielle asked.

"I like to study late at night," Mary told her, "then I sometimes take naps during the day. I'm working on two master's degrees at once."

Danielle thought she knew the type, conscientious to a fault, a person who would brutalize herself physically because of some sort of extra-strength work ethic. It wasn't overwhelming ambition, a desire to succeed; it was somehow necessary. But Danielle admired this kind of driving force. It was neurotic, but somehow pure, and it had the same overall effect that ambition does. Danielle also felt sorry for anyone who put herself through this.

"I'm very unhappy where I'm living," Mary confided. "It's claustrophobic. But I can't afford anything bigger."

Danielle, of course, was dying to get out of the concrete underground pit. She seized the opportunity. "I hate my place too, why don't we look for a two-bedroom place? We could split expenses. Then I could probably live somewhere above ground."

Danielle's newly suspicious nature, her recent social failures, were setting her up to say no, but the desire to escape life as a mushroom made her bold.

"I like the idea," Mary said. "Don't you have a lease?"

Danielle's lease was month-to-month. So was Mary's. Danielle's ended on the 21st, Mary not until the 1st of the next month.

"We can do it then," Danielle said. "When can we get together to go look?"

"How about Wednesday, after Dr. Alexander's class, make a list of possibilities, I will too, and we'll go look at some then." (College students like to make lists.)

Danielle was elated, no more dark, dank days, no more crickets, no more conversations with herself, although these had their merits. They took their trays up, emptied them in the trash, stacked them on the waiting pile, parted to go their separate ways. "See you Wednesday." As Danielle was walking to her car she ran into Kate.

"Follow me out to my place," Kate said.

"I'm in the lot off Speedway," Danielle called.

"OK, I'll meet you."

Kate had an old rattletrap VW on its last legs. It's easy to follow someone in Tucson traffic. The only people who cut in and out are the newcomers, everyone else waits their turn. It's hot but most people have air conditioned cars, they aren't in any hurry.

They turned out Swan Road north and kept going, right toward the mountains. The mountains still overwhelmed Danielle. They loomed so large she couldn't seem to pay attention to anything else. This mountain was getting closer and closer. The houses were further apart. There were stunted trees Danielle didn't recognize and American willows with graceful tiny leaves creating patterned shadows sharply underneath. The sun was brilliant, burning, the sky deep azure, cloudless. The shadows under the trees looked blue-green, giving even the vegetation a blue tinge. The cactuses studded the open ground like fantasy furniture. A few had flowers. There was yucca growing like a weed, some with long curving stems left in the middle, flowerless.

They turned into a semicircular drive that Danielle hadn't even seen in this beautiful desert setting. The house was an old ranch house, which had seen better days, but was perfectly suited to its surroundings. It had a deep open porch held up unevenly on four by four posts. The house was the same brown as the wood of the plants that grew around it. Kate rented the place; her roommate was a guy, not Stuart, but a friend of Kate's from home. They were just roommates.

Inside was all deep shade and comfort. There was a fireplace in the living room, the couches old and covered with India bedspreads; books in the bookcases, low tables, and Mexican rugs on the floor. It was very neat and clean. Plants hung in the windows. You stepped up into the kitchen. It was an old country kitchen, very beat up but still very clean. They sat at the kitchen table and drank sun tea.

"Carson asked for your phone number," Kate said, "he wants to take you out to dinner. What should I say?"

"Oh give it to him," Danielle told her. "He probably won't call anyway." She wanted to know more about him, but didn't want Kate to know that she did.

They talked about school and Kate's work.

"I really need to get a part time job," Danielle said. Her checkbook looked sick.

"Go to the college placement office," Kate said. "They have lots of part-time jobs."

"Oh God, I never thought of that," Danielle groaned. "I think I'll stop in there tomorrow."

"Have you eaten any Mexican food?" Kate asked.

"Nope, I haven't eaten out at all except in the college cafeteria," Danielle admitted.

"It's delicious," Kate said. "I know this place, we'll go for lunch someday, OK?"

"No problem," Danielle answered, the word "go" worked like a magic charm these days. Danielle was glad to go anywhere, especially if she didn't have to go alone.

Kate's roommate "Butch" came in then. They exchanged a few words about who was supposed to do the dishes. Apparently, typical of a lot of male roommates Danielle had known, Butch had just about ceased taking any active interest in housework.

Danielle felt awkward, "I gotta go," she said. "I have reading to do."

"No need," Kate told her, "I have to talk to him when I see him, he's not here very often."

"That's OK, I have to go anyway." Danielle said her good-byes and headed back towards town, leaving the little ranch, the now purple shadows and the looming mountain still an afterimage in her mind's eye. How could she ever have thought the desert was colorless? So many colors assaulted her she wished she could paint it the way she saw it, but she had tried, she knew she couldn't. It would be there in her head, perfect, but her hand couldn't reproduce what her eyes took in. What appeared on the paper or the canvas never had the beauty of what she saw.

As she drove she thought about hippies. All the hippies of ten years ago must have gone to Tucson. That was definitely a style that suited the place. Everyone wore jeans and looked like they had pot stashed in a jar on their coffee table or in their backpack or under the seat of their truck. It was a style Danielle felt comfortable with even though she had decided she didn't like chemicals.

Kate looked like a hippie, the original 60's variety. She was a pretty girl, tall with a tanned well-proportioned body and good features that blended well, nothing too large or too small, eyes, nose, mouth, cheekbones all blended to a harmonious whole. She had long, straight brown hair. She wore cotton imported tops with her jeans. She was the kind of girl you could have hated if she hadn't been so unpretentious. Danielle refused to spend any more of her time being jealous of pretty women.

Closer to town she saw the transients gathered in groups in the parks. It was the perfect climate for it, easy to live outside on almost any day or night of the year. They dressed in the style of the 60's too except they seemed to prize the desert dust enough to save up large quantities of it on their persons. They kept their backpacks with them as they sat alone or in circular groups on the grass. These, however, were not the flower children of the 60's. They dressed the same, looked the same, but they did not have the philosophy of peace, love and happiness, of live and let live, of learning to live in the here and now that Danielle remembered from the 6O's. This was strictly a drug culture, these street corner 'cronies'. It was every man for himself and although temporary, informal alliances might be formed they were not to be trusted. Betrayal was commonplace if expedient. Danielle felt safe in her blue metal isolation booth.

Tucson, to Danielle's senses, was Syracuse, only sunnier and dryer. It was about the same size, with the same dying downtown, the same residential character and the same habit of being ten years behind the times. She thought of a movie she had once seen where space travelers ended up on another earth, except it wasn't earth, it was anti-earth, a mirror earth, earth inside out. She thought she knew how they felt. These were her thoughts without the mountains to distract her. They carried her back to the dingy deeps, Class Insectiva.

The next day Danielle found the student placement office. It was a tiny office way in the back of an inconspicuous building to the right of Old Main. (That was the name of the building Danielle saw the first day.) There was an application that had to be filled out, then you went through a file and pulled out cards of jobs that interested you. After that you were on your own. Danielle copied down several names, addresses and phone numbers of places she wanted to contact. Danielle was not a prime candidate for an office job. She typed 13 WPM. She didn't have much hope, but she wrote down jobs involving office work. The one she wanted most was called "Sonora Safari: Desert Tours." They needed a general office girl, no typing involved. The proprietor's name was Perez Admenihaj. He sounded like a real colorful character. Danielle called for an appointment. She would come to wish that she had never heard of the man. But she was right about the interesting part. She was due to arrive back in the thick of it now.

8
Tucson

Perez was every bit as colorful a character as Danielle imagined, but also very human. He was a small, dark-skinned man, wiry with hyperactive energy, great smile, bad teeth. He was a natural salesman and a natural leader. He collected people who were animated by the electrical charges he gave off. The business, he explained had two parts, the shop itself and the tour division. The shop catered to all kinds of desert interests from hiking to camping, from hunting with a camera to hunting with shotguns and rifles. There was clothing for hot days and cold nights: T-shirts, canvas pants, padded vests and jackets, even safari-style clothes for those who wanted a pseudo-African adventure and could afford expensive play-acting, complete with costumes. There were all kinds of cowboy boots, work boots and lightweight canvas boots. There were hats and belts and neckerchiefs and backpacks. Even pith helmets. There were snakebite kits, snake books, bird books, cactus books, lizard books, maps. There were tents, camp stoves, lanterns, camp stools, cots, sleeping bags. It was a great shop, every corner filled.

The office was a mess. Perez was no bookkeeper. Although he had a rudimentary sense of organization he could barely write and Danielle suspected that reading was not his strong point either. He didn't really interview her. He took her card that said she was from the college, sat her down behind the desk and started showing her the "system". There were envelopes thumbtacked to the walls. There was one for each day of the week. Tour orders went in the envelopes. There were maps on the walls with the tour routes highlighted. There were paid and unpaid receipts everywhere albeit all organized by number and date. Danielle wouldn't plan tours; she would refer the calls to Perez or the tour guy,

Fred or take a message until one of them could get back to the callers. Instead, Danielle would write the number of each receipt, the date and the amount in a monthly account book to be delivered to the tax accountant, bill people who had not paid, prepare payroll checks complete with tax withholding and Social Security. She would also answer the phone and sometimes work as a counter person in the shop. Danielle would only work part time, about twenty hours a week. This was a new business, just starting out. Perez had two silent partners. He had bought a large stock of goods on consignment. He couldn't stay in the store. He needed to get out in the town, to see and be seen, he knew his strengths.

Somewhere halfway through the "system" Danielle realized she had the job. Now she wasn't sure she wanted it. She was attracted and repelled by Perez. He was both magnetic and pathetic. He was either going to be a great seat-of-the-pants success or a total disaster. Danielle could already taste the latter. She was used to picking losers. She felt comfortable here. After all it was just a part time job. You're supposed to be lucky in life if you're unlucky in love. That old adage had held true for Danielle so far. The wisdom of the ancients was about to be tested again.

Danielle left Sonora Safari unsure whether she was elated or just feeling the after effects of Perez-adrenaline. She was glad to have a job, it would help financially, but she felt a bit like she had just taken an accidental ride on a roller coaster. Out of consideration for her fear of heights and her secret desire to bring back the Model A, Danielle never went on roller coasters by choice. However, at the moment a roller coaster ride seemed just the ticket. "The best way out of a fear is through it," more 60's wisdom, by way of Confucius, et al.

Danielle went to class. That brought her back to earth. She got back to the downstairs dive about 9:30. She was tired and not at all ready for the phone when it rang. It was Carson Donahue.

"Hello Danielle, this is Carson, Carson Donahue, Kate's friend."

"Oh hi Carson, yes I remember." (who me?, remember the subject of several recent fantasies?) "What's up?"

"Well I thought, well I wondered, if you'd like to go to dinner Saturday?"

Here it was, the always awkward moment. After all it was just a first date, better yet a meeting, an interview. But things always got so complicated after that. Danielle usually was either attracted immediately or not interested. She knew if she accepted the first time that meant this was the attracted-immediately variety and that all kinds of possible joy and eventual heartbreak were in store. Life was so peaceful when this wasn't happening and so boring. In water Danielle was a wader; in love, a diver. She held her breath and went for it.

"That sounds nice. Is it a fancy place? (She already knew the answer)."

"No, wear jeans, it's a real homey place. I eat there a lot. They've got a prime rib and crab leg dinner. That's what I always get. The crab leg is huge, you won't believe it. I'll pick you up at 7:30, OK?"

"Sure," Danielle said, "I'll be ready."

(A moment of silence)

"Well, see you then," Carson said. "Bye."

"Bye." Danielle thought he should have said "adios", but his "bye" did have a little extra twang to it.

Now Danielle started to worry, she still wasn't on solid food. She had graduated to vegetable and cream soups, and sometimes bread and cheese would go down in small amounts with lots of mayonnaise to smooth the way. She was not at all sure what she would do faced with a prime rib and a giant crab leg across the table from an almost handsome, almost cowboy. In fact, she wasn't in the habit of eating with anyone except Mary at the cafeteria. Oh well, cowboys probably thought women were dainty eaters anyway. And they probably had doggie bags even in Tucson.

Danielle turned on the TV. It was 10:00. She wasn't used to the time zone changes. Prime time ended at 10:00 here. That's when the news came on. Danielle loved to listen to that song they played after the news, "I'd rather be in Tucson, than anywhere I know" with saguaros in the background. After she pledged allegiance to Tucson she turned off the TV and went to bed with her books (that is, after she did the nightly search for crickets and, her newest worry, scorpions).

Danielle and Mary had talked on Wednesday about the apartments in the paper but Danielle had the job interview with Perez and Mary had to see a professor. They put off the search. They tried to get together several times after that but they were busy now. Danielle decided to look by herself. She had the lists they had made. She saw about four places, they were all wrong: too small, too expensive, too dirty. The last place she looked at was on North Swan Road. Danielle loved it before she even got there because you drove towards the mountains. The apartments were set up like a Syracuse motel. All in row, all connected; they formed four lines arranged in a rectangle. In the center was a concrete patio, separated from the concrete sidewalk by rows of planters with shrubbery, flowering bushes, and lacy wrought iron grillwork. The sidewalk ran under a breezeway and formed the perimeter of the rectangle. In the middle of the patio was a large, very clean pool with a blue flowered Mexican tile lining, and a diving board at one end. At the other end broad stairs descended into the pool. There was a pool house at the diving board end of the pool and a chain link fence around the pool area. There was plenty of room for the chaise lounges the complex provided. On the patio, outside the chain link fence, were round white wrought iron patio tables with umbrellas and white wrought iron armchairs with turquoise vinyl cushions.

Danielle didn't want to see the apartment. She was afraid she would hate it. She knew she was going to rent the place;

she thought Mary would be mad, but she couldn't help herself. Unless the apartment was really awful. It wasn't. It needed some cleaning, the furniture was cheap motel tacky; plaid couch, peppery rug, huge lamps with yellowed coolie-hat-shaped shades; stained, paper-thin veneer-covered particle board coffee table and end tables; Formica dining table with chrome chairs, flowered plastic cushions bolted on. But it was huge and it was above ground and it had two bedrooms and a real pool (not a tank). Danielle signed the lease, paid the deposit and went to face the music. Danielle often did things like this. She liked to think she was impulsive but she suspected she just liked to be in control.

Danielle called Mary. She wasn't in. She left a message with the family she boarded with to have her call.

On Saturday Danielle worked her first day at Sonora Safari. She had a quiet day. Perez gave her some hurried instructions and then he left, something about lunch at Lydia's Cafe. Fred was in the store behind the counter, reluctantly taking care of walk-in business. Perez didn't have a cash register, just a cash drawer with a little key that Fred had to use between each transaction. Perez wanted the drawer locked at all times when not in use. All receipts were handwritten. The store was strictly a cash business for now. Perez was checking into credit cards.

Danielle spent the whole afternoon sitting at the littered, dusty old office table, one of the massive old-fashioned kind with a dull finish and bleached moisture rings in haphazard overlapping patterns. She dutifully wrote the receipt numbers, dates and amounts chronologically in the appropriate spots and either recorded a Pd. or left the last space blank as designated on the receipt. (Apparently some people were allowed to postpone payment.) Manner of payment, check or cash had to be recorded and check number if necessary. In between Danielle answered the phone. A guy named Jake dropped in. He seemed surprised to see Danielle. Danielle didn't like him much. He was a small, young guy; both skinny and short, with weasely eyes and long, greasy, dirty blond hair. His most attractive feature was his mouth with the dark blond mustache softening the overall effect of the rest of the face. He plopped himself down in the chair in front of the vacant office desk (a giant old wooden model from the same used office furniture set as the table Danielle was using.)

"Where's Perez?"

"He's at lunch."

"Oh well, I'll wait."

Danielle wasn't happy about this, she wasn't even sure it was acceptable but Fred seemed to take it for granted, he even came in and talked with this Jake character for a few minutes. After Fred went back into the shop Jake kept interrupting Danielle, asking her questions. Nosy guy. Too bad he didn't run the interview, she thought, vaguely annoyed. But it must have been OK because Perez came bouncing back in shortly thereafter, bantered a bit with Danielle, looked at the account book and shook his head yes, grabbed his messages and left with Jake. Fred would lock up, Danielle could go home. "See you Tuesday."

She still had two and a half hours to get ready to go to dinner with Carson. She hadn't even had time to get nervous yet. Danielle decided to turn on some music and take a leisurely bath. It had taken several weeks to get the bathtub into a condition where it seemed safe to actually sit in it for any extended period of time. Danielle was proud of her efforts with bleach and blowtorch. She could really enjoy the dim den now that she could see the light glimmering weakly from the new apartment with two picture windows on No. Swan Rd. She listened to Bob Dylan **Knockin' on Heaven's Door** to get in the mood.

Wrapped in her bathrobe Danielle sang along as loud as she dared with Joni, **Help Me.** She arranged the mirror on the bed and put on makeup. The hair was easy; she just fluffed it up with a long-toothed pick. Danielle planned to break the Tucson fashion rules and wear a dress, barelegged with sandals. She was proud of the slight golden brown color that she was turning. She loved the sun; she had come miles to melt in it. It relaxed her, it was sensuous, and cheerful. She hardly ever pictured herself in the hot sun in a hammock with the blood running down from her wrists anymore.

She turned off the tapes; she needed to calm down. Singing made her feel high. She turned on the TV and picked up a textbook. A little reading would settle her down. Carson was on time. He knocked on the door at 7:30. Danielle didn't invite him in.

"I'm ready, let's go," Danielle said.

He opened the passenger door of the truck but didn't stay to watch as she tried to giant step up in her most feminine, yet modest manner.

"Where is this place?" Danielle said as they left the parking area.

"Across the river," Carson told her.

He meant the Rillito River. Danielle wouldn't have even known it was a river except for the sign near the riverbed which labeled the sandy stretch as the Rillito River. Everyone told her that after a thunderstorm it could become a roaring flood, very dangerous for the unsuspecting driver. Danielle had never seen a drop of water in it. It hadn't rained at all since she'd been here.

"We're going the back way on the River Road," Carson said.

"I can't believe how many places around here are named for water," Danielle said. "It seems crazy to live in the desert if you long for open bodies of water."

"There really is water in all those places sometimes," Carson said.

"What kind of work do you do?" Danielle asked, not wanting to sound like she was prying, not wanting to be mundane, but she hadn't been able to picture Carson actually working, except maybe herding cattle.

"I do framing," Carson said. "I'll show you the house we're doin' now. Jim's workin' on the same job. There's lots of construction work here, they're buildin' all over the place, 'specially off River Road."

He pulled into a flat dirt lot with the raw fresh two by fours of a half-framed house rising from a concrete slab.

"No basement," Danielle said.

"They don't use basements much here," Carson said.

Danielle couldn't believe her luck living in one of the few basements in all of Tucson.

"There's no cactus here," Danielle said. "Where do they get all the cactus to use for landscaping. First they take it all out, then they have to buy it back?"

"Landscaping is a big business here. That's what Stuart does. Stuart's honest but lots of guys go out in the desert at night and pirate saguaros and sell them illegally. They get caught a lot though," Carson told her.

They were north of the river, near where Kate lived; Danielle recognized it from the proximity to the mountains. They went east on the River Road. Houses were sparser here; the desert seemed unpeopled, the houses, which were built to blend in with the landscapes, difficult to spot.

"There's a roadrunner," Carson said, pointing ahead of them.

Danielle saw it, crossing the road, running into the parking lot of a supermarket. Roadrunner and parking lot, it seemed a bizarre paradox. Where was Wiley Coyote? They turned north on Sabino Canyon Road.

"This is a great place," Carson said. I eat here a lot after work."

He pulled the truck into a parking place right in front of the restaurant as if he was pulling into his own driveway. 'The Hidden Valley Inn and Restaurant' Danielle read.

She liked the place; it was comfortable, but attractive. The tables had white linen cloths and candles, the chairs had arms. There were booths under corral cut arches. The waitresses knew Carson. They got a table immediately. Danielle looked around at the other diners. There was a mix of people; some dressed up, some obviously just coming from work although they had spruced up a bit. There were families and couples, and friendly, more amorphous groups. It was a popular place.

Carson ordered a Coors for each of them without consultation. It didn't seem an insensitive thing to do, he obviously did not imagine that Danielle would want any other beverage. She already knew she would have to order the prime rib and crab leg, so she did.

"How long have you known Kate and Stuart?" Danielle asked.

"I've known Stuart about ten years but I've only known Kate about two. They're good people," Carson told her.

It made Danielle cringe when someone said 'they're good people' but she overlooked this first flaw. It was not the "get out of here fast type." Only semantics, she decided.

"Don't you miss New York?" Carson asked her.

"Some parts. I miss my family, and I miss the trees. We have a cottonwood tree in our backyard. When a storm is coming all the leaves turn over and the whole tree looks silver against the dark gray-blue sky. Sometimes New York is so green on a sunny day, even on a gloomy day in August it's so lush and rich. I love the trees and the light. Tucson doesn't have that soft filtered light. I can't describe it but I can see it."

Danielle stopped. She realized she sounded homesick, which she was. But she hadn't even begun to get sick of the desert. She shifted the shutter back to the more austere beauty of here and now.

Their dinner came. Danielle was shocked. She had never eaten a crab leg. All the crabs she had seen were small; the ones she, Nicole and Audrey Ann had caught in Ocracoke were tiny by comparison. This one had to be from the grandfather (or grandmother) of crabs. It had to be eighteen

71

inches long and two inches around at the wide end. And the prime rib wasn't small either. Now Danielle was really in trouble. Surely her inability to eat would be a bit conspicuous in the face of such bounty.

Danielle did her best; the crab was delicious, tender and sweet, dipped in the clarified butter; the prime rib, the perfect companion. But when she was done it looked like she had hardly touched it. Carson didn't seem to notice. He had ordered an astonishing number of Coors refills, most of which Danielle avoided by sipping slowly, but he acted the same as he had before. Coors seemed to have no effect on him. Even his kidneys seemed to be holding up. Danielle had coffee after dinner, Carson had another Coors.

"There's this place out in the desert that I know you'd really like. I'll have to take you there," Carson said.

Danielle would have been pleasantly surprised but she was used to this male trait. Men always were infatuated at first, that is if they were attracted at all. They always made mad plans about all the wonderful things they wanted to do with you. They had probably fantasized about doing them with someone and there you were, someone. Later they would usually back off though.

"That would be nice," Danielle said carefully.

Her doggie bags came and they left.

"Let's take a drive," Carson said. "I'll show you the land Stuart and I own on the Rillito."

It wasn't far, they listened to music on the way, country, of course. *"Desperado, come down off your fences and open the gate."* Southwestern invitation.

It was very dark; Danielle noticed the stars for the first time. You could see thousands, even the very dim ones. She wanted to lay down and just look up but 1) the relationship was too new for the posture and 2) she remembered the cactus. The land was a wild, unimproved piece, but it was on the empty river. Danielle recognized the real estate value of the location. Carson talked about the horses they wanted to put on the land.

He took her hand and they walked back to the truck. No doubt-the excitement was there. But he was a perfect gentleman. He took her home, walked her to the door, gave her a polite little kiss. He did say he'd call. Then he mounted his big red steed and rode off into the night. Heigh ho, Danielle.

It was Sunday again. Danielle felt out of balance, her recent patterns all out of synch. She went to the library. It was almost midterm. She had exams to study for. By the time she came back to the underground hacienda her rhythms were restored.

Monday she saw Mary. At first, when she found out about the apartment, Mary was a bit cool. In fact, she was angry. She felt Danielle had been inconsiderate. She didn't back out but she didn't share Danielle's pleasure either. They sat next to each other in class taking notes, waiting for the lecture to end. It was a long one. After class, when Danielle took Mary to see the apartment, Mary started to thaw. They saw the manager and Mary added her signature to the lease. It was official. Danielle had an above-ground address.

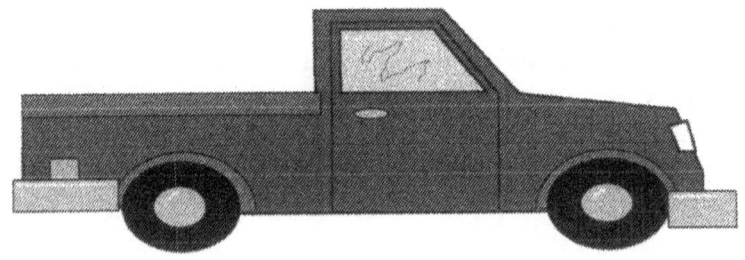

9
Tucson

Kate called. She wanted Danielle to go to lunch and sample some Mexican food. She was also dying to know what happened on the date with Carson. Danielle didn't have to work and her class was later that evening. Kate picked her up around 12:30. The old VW was not doing well but Kate wanted to drive. She knew where they were going, besides she was the better driver.

It was an elegant place, El Parador on Broadway. The restaurant was in a brick courtyard filled with all kinds of tropical and desert plants. On both sides of the courtyard arched doorways led into exclusive shops. Kate ordered a pitcher of margaritas. Danielle liked the idea.

Kate talked Danielle into ordering chicken enchiladas, Kate had chili rellenos. The amenities taken care of, Danielle knew it was time for the third degree. Danielle obliged without coercion offering an edited account of the big night.

"But what did you talk about?" Kate wondered.

"I don't remember," Danielle said, not wanting to go through it all. "I guess we talked about Tucson and Carson's job, we didn't seem to have a lot of trouble talking."

"I really like Carson as a person," Kate said, "but I really don't think you two have a lot in common. He's not looking for a serious relationship, Danielle. I think you better take it easy."

"Sure," Danielle said absentmindedly. Kate knew Carson pretty well and she was an honest and caring person. She knew she should listen to Kate. She knew she wouldn't.

"How's your job," Kate said, mercifully changing the subject.

"My boss, Perez. I don't know about that guy. I like him but he's a strange one," Danielle said. "He's got a terrible self-image. He's always doing things for all the wrong reasons. He's dating an 18-year-old girl. He must be about 40. And he brags about her. He's so proud of her. She's a pretty girl, a nice, simple, down-home girl, tall with long dark blonde hair but they have kind of a stormy relationship. I don't think she's going to stay with him. I think she's attracted by his energy and his position. He makes people think he's special, while all the time he thinks he's worthless. I should look for another job. I have a bad feeling about this guy. But he's so interesting."

"Geez, if you feel that way, you ought to list the job with the school again and get someone to replace you," Kate said.

Danielle knew Kate was right again, but she didn't think she was going to do that yet. The roller coaster headed for the top of the track.

They were three-quarters of the way through the pitcher. Kate's food was long gone. Danielle loved the enchiladas, they were delicious, but eating was still not her forté. She had eaten about one-third of the lunch and then quit. But she was starting to feel really good from those delicious margaritas.

"I got an apartment," Danielle told Kate about the new place and her roommate, Mary.

"How are you going to move," Kate asked. "You can't fit that chair you bought in your Toyota, can you?"

Danielle hadn't given it much thought, being so happy to leave her nocturnal niche.

"I'll borrow the truck from Stuart and we can do it all in one trip," Kate offered.

She was always doing things like that. Danielle never ceased to be amazed by Kate's generosity and her stability. It made Danielle feel beholden, but it also made her feel at home.

"Thanks Kate, God you're always so nice. Don't you ever worry about people taking advantage."

"You'd do the same for me," Kate said.

But Danielle wasn't sure that she would take a stranger under her wing like that. In fact she was pretty sure she wouldn't. Possibly once she would have, not now.

"Come on let's get out of here," Danielle said, "while I can still walk." It's true that margaritas go down real easy on a hot day eating hot food, but Danielle wasn't used to drinking half a pitcher for lunch. However, when the heat dropped down on her just outside the door of the restaurant, she suddenly felt perfectly sober. Kate never had seemed affected by the alcohol at all.

"We have a friend who's playing in a group at a night club," Kate said. "I'll get Carson to take you and you can go with Stuart and me."

Danielle didn't point out that Kate's messages were mixed, she just said,

"OK, if Carson agrees."

"I've been meaning to ask you," Kate said as she drove Danielle home, "does anyone ever call you Danni?"

"Yes, and I've missed hearing it."

"Good, Danielle's too long," Kate said. They arrived at Danielle's apartment. "Tell me when you're ready to move."

Danielle waved goodbye and went inside to get ready for class.

Perez was at the shop when Danielle got to work the next day. And he had no appointments. He was going to stay and get in her hair the whole time. He paced around the office, lifting things from one spot and putting them down in another. He waited on customers in the shop. He showed Danielle the picture of Gina for the eightieth time. Finally he sat down in the chair in front of the desk and drank a cup of coffee which he didn't need. He told Danielle the story of his life, in between phone calls. His mother was of Spanish descent living in Puerto Rico, his father, a sailor from India. They met, but they shouldn't have. His mother's father was in shipping. She was on the docks momentarily unattended. She was a gently raised young woman and this was an unlikely occurrence. They fell in love but the romance was forbidden. They saw each other furtively on several of his father's shore leaves. They eloped and married. Perez was the result. His father died at sea and his mother had to raise him alone. She was an outcast to her family, she never saw them, they never helped her. He came to America as soon as he was old enough to hop a ship. Danielle didn't know if she believed it but it was a very sad story.

Sylvia and Frank stopped by. They were an attractive, affluent middle-aged couple, both retired, both seeking "new experiences." They were drawn to the kinky and quirky although they were neither. Perez was both; he was right up their alley. They had their RV parked in the lot at the shop. Soon they were off to San Diego. They wanted Perez to have dinner with them but he had to go to the bank. He decided that Danielle could close up and go to the bank on the way home. He showed her how to fill out the bank deposit slip for the cash and then the checks. Danielle didn't really want the responsibility but she was the hired help. That was the first of many times she waited in the long, hot line at the auto-drive-up window of The Arizona Bank.

Danielle had been trying to borrow the apartment manager's vacuum cleaner for days. Her rug had terminal lint. For some reason the vacuum cleaner was as elusive as a cool day in the desert. She couldn't sit down with all that white stuff all over the rug. Every time she tried to read her peripheral vision tricked her brain into believing that those white flecks were moving. She fired up her semi-retired J.C. Penney card, checked her make up, changed her shoes and headed out. Halfway up the stairs from the cement cricket cemetery she heard the phone ring. Once - she fumbled with her keys, twice - she was in the door. She picked it up on the third ring. It was Carson.

"Hello Danielle, this is Carson Donahue."

"Hi Carson, how are you?"

"I hurt my back, been out of work a couple of days. Went back today?"

"How was it?"

"All fixed, no problem. What are you up to?"

"Not much, I was just going shopping."

"What are you doing Saturday?"

"No plans, why what's up?"

"Thought you might like to go see this group with Stuart and Kate. This friend of ours plays guitar, just a small club, nothing fancy."

"What kind of music do they play?"

"It's sort of country rock. Wear jeans."

(Danni could have predicted that.) "OK, what time?"

"I'll come get you about 7:30, you can have dinner at my house."

"All right, see you then. Bye."

"Bye," Carson said with the twang still intact.

Danielle didn't know why, but Carson made her nervous, excited. Of course, it was never an explainable phenomenon. Why should such diverse elements produce such an interesting chemical reaction? Couldn't electricity and compatibility exist simultaneously? Danielle guessed the two states were almost contradictory. When they did coincide the circuit often burned out quickly although the light it gave off was said to be very bright. Oh well, these explorations in physics never did make a whole lot of sense, and they were very taxing. After all she had almost failed the course. At best, all she ever arrived at was a set of poorly mixed metaphors. She knew that in spite of her reservations she was going ahead, at least, on with it. Danielle went to J.C. Penney to buy a vacuum. She at least knew how to deal with white lint on the carpet.

Sonora Safari had become very familiar very quickly. Everything that happened there seemed to happen right around her desk. It was very entertaining and Danielle loved feeling at the center of things. Every time she was there a collection of characters was hanging about waiting for Perez, or chatting with Perez, or analyzing Perez, trying to get a grip on his unquestionable, but incomprehensible charisma. Perez wandered in and out of it smiling and joking, needing love from everyone. Perhaps that was the key to the whole thing. He was so needy.

On this Saturday Danielle had just opened up and settled down to work. Fred was sitting on the other side of the office until time for the day's tour. The Sonora Safari Cherokee was all packed up, gassed up and quietly grazing. Danielle didn't hear anyone come in but suddenly someone was in front of the desk. She looked up and up some more. He was tall, dark and handsome, with a slim athletic look and a boyish grin. He had on a cowboy hat. But somehow Danielle did not find him attractive, she recognized that he was gorgeous but her heart did not fall into her shoes, her tongue did not tie itself in knots. He was looking for Perez. He was one of the "silent" partners. The door opened and a woman entered, tall, long dark hair, pretty face, a big woman but very well dressed, nice looking. Her husband was Chet, she was Ginger.

"What's happening? Isn't Perez here? Who are you?"

Danni introduced herself and explained her function.

"Perez told us to meet him here at 9:30. Has he called?"

"No, but if he told you to be here he's probably on his way."

Danielle didn't want to let on that Perez had no concept of time, but apparently his habits were well known by these two. Perez came dashing in, panic in his eyes only momentarily, then he recovered his usual cheerful manner.

"Did you meet Danni?" Yeah, well then, let's go. We'll get some breakfast and talk. Danielle, we'll be at Lydia's. Everything under control here? Of course it is. I'll be back in time for the tour. Let's go man."

Danielle raised her eyebrows to Fred behind their disappearing backs. No response. Fred, a stolid conservative guy, rarely registered any response to any of the bizarre things that went on at Sonora Safari. It was a lot like being alone when he was there. But he was dependable and Danielle guessed that's why she was there too. It was either great business acumen or dumb luck that drove Perez to hire people who were the exact polar opposites of himself. Danielle didn't see the unlikely trio return, nor did she see the tour depart. She only worked until two that day. It was difficult to imagine what went on at SS and DT when she was not there. It seemed to her as unreal as **Brigadoon** , only appearing at intervals, those being when she, Danielle, was present. However when she had to decipher the scrawls on the receipts Perez wrote, it brought her back from this rather egocentric view of reality.

Her little blue Toyota carried her across town into the bowels of the earth to do some studying and to get ready for the date with Carson. Well not the date, that word was out of use, the evening (just right, properly noncommittal).

She waltzed around her living room floor in her bathrobe, suddenly nervous that they might have to do the country swing. She didn't know how to do the country swing. She never could follow. She had gotten kicked out of ballroom dance class for giggling before they ever got to the "following" part. To tell the truth, although she loved to dance alone around her apartment and had taken four years of ballet, she did not know how to dance with anyone if you had to hold on, if you had to coordinate your movements with those of someone else.

Since she didn't have a bedroom separate from the living room and a below ground bathroom is hardly conducive to romantic fantasy or leisurely primping she could not really afford to keep "her man" waiting as the classic advice to young women growing up in the 50's had suggested, so Danni was ready when Carson knocked on the door. She had decided to avoid a further statement of her individuality and to wear blue jeans. That way at least she knew no one could disapprove of her clothing, in case she had to make a fool of herself in other ways and attempt dancing. Her top was a variation on an Indian bedspread, very Tucson. Carson seemed to approve. He opened the passenger door of the red Chevy and let her climb in on her own again, obviously not realizing that to such a short person a pick-up cab is some climb.

"How's school going?" Carson asked politely.

"Midterms just got over," Danielle answered, just as politely.

They were awkward, a bit stiff with each other. They didn't have any memories together; they couldn't share a silence.

"How'd you do?"

"No problem," Danielle said. "I don't have anything really difficult this semester. I did OK. How's work? Any more problems with your back?"

"Nope, framed a whole house this week. It hurts a little tonight though."

They lapsed into silence riding out Speedway northwest again. Everyone Danielle had met seemed to live in that quarter near Sabino Canyon and the river.

"What did you cook for dinner?" Danielle asked, a little worried.

"Havelina stew," Carson said.

Now Danielle was afraid to show her ignorance but even more nervous about eating something with a name she didn't recognize. Carson helped her out.

"Havelina is a wild pig," he said. "I got him when I was huntin' one day. I took him and had him butchered. Already ate most of the meat, just some odds and ends left. One was a package of stew meat."

Wild pig stew, Danielle sent up a silent prayer for help. "Please make it edible."

They pulled into the driveway of a little house on a street Danielle didn't know. Tucson was full of little one-story stucco houses like this one. The door was off to one side of a front porch that was full of tools, a big table saw, old and new lumber. No little wicker chairs with flowered cushions here. The living room was functional and, if not clean, at least picked up. There was little attempt to coordinate the various couches; chairs, lamps and tables although they all did share the same general shabbiness and a gold and brown color scheme did sort of predominate. Carson had built in some nice pine shelves on the front wall, these held some magazines, the TV, a plastic alarm clock and some empty wine bottles with candles, along with an old clock set into the side of a replica clipper ship. Lots of coins, coin wrappers, nail clippers, combs and other assorted pocket contents had probably been placed there when the guys cleaned their pockets because those things had no designated spot. A cardboard painting of deer grazing near a small desert stream hung on the wall over the gold couch where it had been designed to fit. A mystery apparatus on a small table in front of the easy chair turned out to be a bullet stuffer. Danielle was getting a glimpse into the inner workings of cowboydom or hood or whatever. Now she understood that it was not the environmental urge not to litter the desert that had them scouring the hard packed desert floor for bullet casings that day of the breakfast. It was the cowboy brand of efficient housekeeping. (After all, now that she thought about it they had left all the Coors cans right where they fell or stood.) The only feminine touch in the entire room was a macramé enclosed hanging plant between the kitchen and the living room. The plant was drooping and leggy, dusty and coughing, on its last legs. Carson explained that it was left over from his last live-in girlfriend.

For some unexplained reason Danielle did not pick up on this last remark and run with it as she was usually driven to do. She wasn't even tempted to pump for details, name, face and figure. She vaguely wondered what was happening to her. Was mental health setting in, or perhaps she wasn't even anticipating any permanence in this relationship? She didn't need to ask Carson, she could ask Kate.

Actually Jim, Carson's cryptic and, (Danielle imagined), terribly innocent roommate was cooking the stew in a surprisingly neat and large kitchen. It had been simmering all day in a crock-pot of all things. It actually looked edible and smelled delicious.

Carson opened a Coors for everyone, introduced Danielle again to Jim.

"Call me Danni," she said.

She saw Carson react.

"You too, Carson" she said. To Jim she said, "that stew smells good.

He blushed so red that she withdrew any thoughts of starting a conversation. They ate out of bowls in the living room in front of the TV. Danni could take her time eating. She started to actually enjoy the taste of the rich stew and the Coors. Hunters obviously took all aspects of their work seriously. They even watched Marlin Perkins. He was talking about raptors; eagles and hawks, where they lived, how they hunted, the dangers DDT was presenting to their survival.

Danni felt good. She felt like she was back home listening to her brother David and his friend Miles plan their next hunting trip. Only this time she was right in the room with them instead of eavesdropping from her bedroom across the hall. She didn't care the least about hunting but the camaraderie shared by David, Miles and Pete, the dog; their total absorption in their plans; their obvious animation had always left her feeling lonely, uncommitted. She didn't know of a single interest she had that she could share so intimately and enjoyably with someone else. Here she was "inside" the forbidden bedroom with Miles and David (and Pete), on however ad hoc a basis. She found she was smiling.

Carson caught her eye and smiled with her. He didn't know why she was smiling but he seemed pleased that she was. She felt close to him for that moment. After that last quiet communication everyone suddenly burst into action. They all got up and carried their plates into the kitchen. As a guest Danni felt duty-bound to offer to do the dishes although she didn't want to set any precedents just in case. But Jim said absolutely not, he was going to do the dishes. Carson, of course, didn't say anything.

When Danni went into the bathroom she almost gagged, she almost waited until they got to the bar, but she couldn't. This was an unloved, much used bathroom. There was dirt in every corner, there were tiny brown hairs stuck to the sink back. The tub, which she concluded was used only for its shower, had never known Clorox. It seemed that here was a job these two guys considered unnecessary, or at least beneath the talents of skilled laborers. Danni levitated her way through the bathroom. She had made a silent promise that if she continued to see Carson she was not going to try to introduce even a modicum of beauty into the surroundings, she would take it as she saw it, but now she had to modify her vow. Perhaps, in self-defense, she might have to do a little something with the bathroom, just maybe sneak in a sponge, some steel wool, a gallon bottle of Lysol, do a little scrubbing here and there. Oh well, no sense getting ahead of herself.

They had fun at the bar; the band was pretty good. They played some Marshall Tucker and Alabama and some Charlie Daniels. They danced the way Danni knew how, not touching. They slow-danced a couple of times but Carson was not a fancy ballroom smoothie and it felt good being close, so not being able to follow wasn't too much of a problem. There was a pool table on the bar side of the club. Carson was good. He showed Danni with his fingertip where to hit the ball, then held his finger near the cushion where she would get the right angle. He was a natural physicist, estimating accurately the angle of deflection, the momentum as it passed from one ball to the next. He made Danni feel like a hot pool shooter. Kate and Stuart were easy to be with, they were low key. Nobody got drunk; it was a nice mellow evening.

Carson asked her back to his place for coffee. Danni knew this was "it". She really hadn't ever made a decision about whether she wanted to or not. She let her body make it for her. They rode quietly in the dark Chevy. Carson pulled her over next to him and put his arm around her. She liked it. No questions asked. She guessed a little of the cave woman still lurked in her genetic pool.

They stumbled through the dark porch, the lumpy obstacles distinguishable as darker shapes. Carson actually did make coffee and put on some music. They drank the coffee curled up together on the couch. He pulled her by the hand towards the bedroom. She cast her lot with her hormones for better or for worse. It was pre-intellectual. It was lovely.

In the morning, after a warm lazy replay, Danni, with mindless smile, took stock for the first time of this room that she would see on a number of equally rewarding occasions. It was a bright room, big pine bed dominating the space. There was clutter, but the room was not unclean. Carson had obviously hand-built the bed with fresh thick wood, stained and polished it himself. There was a door across from the bed that led out to the back yard, a wild expanse of tall scrub and dry green weeds that bore some resemblance to grass. Carson had gone to the kitchen, to make fresh coffee. Danni dressed and went in the bathroom, which had not miraculously improved during her absence. She had to go to the library to work on a paper. After the coffee Carson drove her to her apartment. One last kiss at the door and he was gone. No "I'll call you" - not a man to make promises.

It was almost April, Danni couldn't believe so much time had gone by. It was very hot in Tucson already, days in the 90's. The nights were beautiful after the hot days sitting in traffic, walking across the campus, sitting in the unairconditioned office at Sonora Safari. Danni didn't mind this heat, she loved seeing the sun day after day. You didn't have to rush out and use each perfect day, not knowing when the next would arrive. The sun was there every day, warming the world, warming her bones, turning her skin golden. Her mood reflected the lightness of the atmosphere that seemed to rise in thin wavy lines from the sun-baked pavements. In fact the mood of Tucson seemed half-Mexican fiesta, half-American barbecue. People were friendly to total strangers, as they never were in Syracuse, the paranoia and alienation burned away, responses purified in the same natural oven that once baked the adobe bricks. Once when Danni ate lunch in a diner, a middle-aged, middle-class woman, who would have eaten lunch silently in Syracuse, talked with Danni throughout the meal just as if they were not absolutely unacquainted. Danni occasionally thought about staying here when her year was up but she knew she couldn't. She had signed a paper. It she didn't return and teach for a year, she could be prosecuted.

This was the Sunday Danni was moving into her new apartment. She would be up and out of the last dark, damp place left in her present life, up above ground with the bright light and the horizon that seemed to be one hundred miles further away in every direction than it was in New York. She was packed and ready, waiting for Kate. The electric company had been notified. Southwestern Bell had been notified. She still had to return once to clean and turn in her keys but she watched the delicate descendants of another desert knowing she was seeing this exotic scene for the last time.

Kate arrived. It only took one load in the pickup to move all Danni's possessions. She led Kate down Speedway to her new home on No. Swan Rd. pointed straight at the mountain. They unloaded but didn't unpack. Kate had to leave to go to dinner with Stuart, Danni headed back to University Ave. one last time to turn the cellar back over to the crickets. The manager was not home so she left the keys with the woman upstairs and drove happily to her new place, anxious to claim the space and put her personal mark on it.

10
Tucson

Sunlight blazed through the bottoms of the closed slats of Danielle's new bedroom blinds. She propped herself up in the big double bed that came with the place and smiled at the spaciousness of this big bright room. There was a big double dresser with a mirror, there was a large closet, there was even a bookcase. Danni opened the blinds and those indescribable hot-cold, intensely yellow molecules of desert light slammed into Danni's new bedroom. This window looked out at the dusty back driveway and the carport. You couldn't see the mountains. You could see a bit of the side street. You could see an architecturally designed house across the street, modern, angular pine wood boards in patterned facade, fish eye window set into the pine, stucco wings growing from the pined Cyclops tower in different directions and at several levels. Danni decided to take pictures of Tucson houses one day soon. She made sure the blue metal commuter was still tucked in its unaccustomed carport slot and then she went out to putter in her new kitchen.

Danni didn't have any classes until later in the day, she didn't have to work until tomorrow. She wanted to have breakfast on the patio at one of the wrought iron tables. Then she wanted to lay in the sun by the pool with the mountain above and maybe take a swim. But she felt self-conscious, as if everyone would be watching her from behind their identical blinds. She decided to do it anyway. She took a book out to the breakfast table with her coffee. The bushes between the covered walkway and the uncovered patio were jasmine and the smell was wonderful. She wanted to keep walking back and forth, into the fragrance and out, in and out, so that the scent would remain.

The sun was so strong it brought tears to her eyes. It hurt to look at the light grey concrete surfaces around her. It was early and it was already hot. The heat didn't bother her, it was dry heat; it warmed her, but it wasn't heavy. It wasn't at all like the one week in Syracuse when things heated up. Syracuse was the steam bath, Tucson was the sauna.

She saw an apartment door, around the corner from her own, open and a middle-aged man emerge. He was handsome in a big, middle-aged way. He looked like someone who might have danced or played accordion on the Lawrence Welk show. Oh geez, he was headed her way. Danni didn't have room for another person in her morning. It was strictly solo. She was a little annoyed but she smiled at him anyway. She didn't want to have hostile neighbors. He held out his hand. "James," he said, "I'm your neighbor."

"Hi James, I'm Danielle."

"If you need anything, let me know."

Danni didn't think so. He seemed a smarmy character. She felt immediately on her guard. She told herself that she shouldn't make quick judgements like this but she felt like he was flirting. He was, after all, way too old for her. She wanted him to go on about his business.

"You rented this place by yourself?" he asked.

"No," Danni said as formally as she could, "my roommate will be here next week. We're students at the University." He wasn't shy, she thought.

"Gotta run, have to get to work," he said.

Well at least he works, Danni thought, her paradise tarnished. Every paradise has its serpent. But once she had her bathing suit on and the sun had turned her to languid latex on the lounge chair under the mountain by the blue pool the serpent had disappeared. Eden had returned.

Reluctantly Danni gathered her pool paraphernalia and went inside to take a shower and to get ready for her class. Mary was in this class and she knew she would be curious about how Danielle liked the new place. Danielle decided to suggest to Mary that she move in right away. She didn't know why she didn't think of it before. She was paying rent at both places anyway. It shouldn't really matter which place she stayed.

Danielle grabbed her books and went out to the carport. She hadn't had to cover the steering wheel with the towel to keep it cool enough to touch. Oh the wonders of the "classy" life. As she opened the car door a little green lizard darted out from under the front end of the car and up the mint green concrete wall where it clung, almost invisible. Danni smiled at it but it didn't indicate that it felt especially chummy.

Mary liked the idea of moving in right away. She hadn't thought about it but, why not. Danielle agreed to help her move her things before work the next day. When Danni got home Kate was there. She let them both in and showed Kate around.

"God, Danni, it looks like an Econo-Lodge had a sale."

"I know, it really is gross furniture," Danni agreed, "but I don't care, I can live with it."

"My car died," Kate said.

"The Beetle? Are you sure? Can't Stuart fix it?"

"Stuart says to give it a decent burial. Come with me while I look at some used cars."

"Will the VW make it?"

"Just in case, follow me in yours."

"Let me just put this sun tea out on the porch, then we'll go. Where is this place?"

"Over near Miracle Mile."

Danni followed Kate to Earl's Used Cars just off the Miracle Mile. It looked like a real gyp joint. Danni would never have trusted "Earl", if that was his name. But Kate seemed to have supreme confidence. She test drove several cars and immediately settled on a big dark green Buick, about 6 or 7 years old. Danni had no idea how she made her choice. At least they didn't have to worry about rust. "Earl, the squirrel", also gave her a small trade-in amount for the VW. They switched the plates and drove back to Danni's. Kate said she'd take care of the registration the next day. Danni would have had to test drive a dozen cars, then have her father or her brother pass on the car before she could have decided.

Danni brought in the sun tea and they sat at the kitchen table in the shade of the jasmine bushes and drank from tall icy glasses.

"I'm having a party," Kate said, "a backyard barbecue, end of May. It's on a Sunday. I want you to come."

"Is Carson going?" Danni asked.

"Well, he's invited."

"I wonder why he didn't mention it."

"Danni, I don't know about Carson. I hope you don't get too hung up."

Danni thought maybe Kate knew something she wasn't saying but she didn't think she could get it out of her.

"I wonder what Stuart will say about the car," Danni said.

"It doesn't matter, it's my car," Kate said, taking the glasses out to the kitchen. "Gotta go, got a class tonight. I'll talk to you soon."

Danni settled down on her herculon plaid sofa to catch up on her assignments. Then she listened to "I'd rather be in Tucson" and went in the bedroom to read. She was reading **The World According To Garp** and she loved it.

They moved Mary's few belongings in the next day and Danielle left her sitting happily by the pool to go to the madness of Sonora Safari. The minute she got there she could see that Perez was more keyed up than usual. He was really flying high. The country club had hired Sonora Safari to do a big "desert do". They wanted to sponsor a box lunch desert trek complete with party canopies. They would bring the bar. Perez was going to have his picture in the paper and everything. He was talking a mile a minute with that big

Perez smile making him look like a wizened Indian fakir (with a Spanish accent.)

Perez always wore the same (at least it looked like the same) jeans jacket with weathered blue jeans (some embroidered) and a tee shirt. He always had the same dusty boots. Danni wondered if he'd wear that for the photo. As if he read her mind he ran into the shop and came back wearing an electric blue satin baseball jacket.

"Hey, look at this Danni, what you think? Pretty nice, huh?"

He turned around. The Sonora Safari logo was on the front in white.

"And take a look at this-"

Danni couldn't help but smile. He was so excited. He was holding a Sonora Safari tee shirt with a desert sunset and a saguaro and little silhouette people with backpacks. Danni had never seen him so happy.

"And Gina's having her picture taken with me."

Lately Danni had thought that Gina really wanted to be free of Perez. She was always irritated with him. She had a sour puss on her all the time. She only smiled when guys other than Perez talked to her. She had exhibited all the signs of someone who was looking for a way "to leave [her] lover". Perez always was nervous when she was with him at the shop. He looked sad to Danni, and he was overly anxious to please, all his cockiness and bravado gone.

But Danni didn't really blame Gina. She was sure Perez would be hell to have a relationship with unless you had the upper hand. He was so volatile. She was sure the two had physical fights, that there was actual physical violence between them.

Perez's mood swings had been even more noticeable than usual lately. When he was high, he was almost manic; when he was low, his depression was all consuming, he had nothing good to say about himself. He was either borderline psychotic, on drugs, or both.

But today he was happy. As Danni entered numbers in the account book, waited on people in the shop and answered the phone she couldn't help but feel a little lighter. She was glad for Perez. Maybe this would straighten things out for him. Besides it was hard to feel bad when there was a Perez festival passing by.

When Fred came in Perez took Danni to Lydia's for some iced tea. Lydia's was just a little neighborhood diner, not stylish, but comfortable. It contained about five square Formica-topped tables and a Formica-topped lunch counter with stools. The table surfaces were all white flecked with grey, so was the counter top. The chairs didn't all match. There were newspaper articles and prayers and other yellowed pieces of paper posted on the walls. It was clean.

Everybody knew Perez. Nobody made a fuss over Danni. It was like being in somebody's kitchen. Perez bought Danni some soup and a toasted cheese sandwich and carried on a running conversation with everyone in the place all the while she ate. They admired his jacket, they talked greyhound racing, they joked with Perez like family. Danni had never seen Perez so relaxed. He didn't go back to work with her. He had come over in Danni's car. He sent her back to do the bank deposit and wait for closing time. She left him there, bullshitting and happy. The Sonora Safari afternoon dragged on by.

Mary was easy to live with. She was neat, undemanding and she was gone a lot. Since she was going for two master's degrees at once she spent a lot of time at the library. She had two very good friends who were a little different, but very accomplished. They were both slightly older than Mary and Danielle, and Danielle realized that she still saw herself as a girl because, by contrast, they seemed grown women. One of Mary's friends, Janet, reminded Danielle of Judy Collins. She was pretty in a full-hipped earthy sort of way. She was a professor at the University. She was very soft-spoken and very peaceful. She didn't visit often but Mary went to her house. The other friend, Jean was shyer, not as warm, but every bit as intelligent. She seemed extremely old-fashioned because of a rather matronly style. She had a stern belief in what was obviously a very strong moral code. Danielle had difficulty understanding the connection between Jean and Mary.

Mary was more social than Danielle; she seemed to have a childlike anticipation of each event that offered itself, as if it was being experienced for the first time. She could talk to anyone, and her interest in them was real. She stood close to people when she talked, she asked a lot of questions, she was calm, yet interested, except with men she found attractive. Then Mary would become a different person. Her voice would sound hesitant; it would break and crackle. She would actually blush. Danielle was not a world class male devastator, but Mary seemed to find her very stylish and knowledgeable in these matters. She seemed to feel that Danielle had things to teach her about real life, that Danielle was "in touch". Danni was fascinated with this view of herself. She might have come to believe in it, but each time another of her klutzy moves would restore perspective.

Mary and Carson did not even speak the same language. She didn't dislike him, she didn't like him. They almost didn't exist for each other. But somehow the fact that Danni had him was additional proof to Mary of Danielle's social sophistication.

One morning at breakfast Mary shared with Danielle her past life. She had been a nun for about eight years. She had only recently left the sisterhood. All of the pieces fell into place. Her friends were also ex-nuns. Danni wasn't Catholic. But even non-Catholic girls romanticize nuns and go through a phase of religious fervor or fantasy similar to the more secular ballerina phase. Danni had pictured herself in the full black and white everyday habit of the nuns of her youth, in the simple but spotlessly clean brick-floored room at the cloister, with the simple cross on the white washed wall above the twin cot and the rosary beads draped over the bed post or lying in an artistic pool on top of the snowy white linen cloth on the little bedside stand. She had pictured herself walking in measured paces with her votive candle in front, pacing silently with her sisters to vespers in the chapel.

But Mary had really lived it. She had done all of the things of Danni's fantasy or perhaps not quite. She had been a nun all through the seventies. She had worked not in cloister, but out in the world among struggling people. She had worn not the protective robes of the fifties but the short, far less romantic garb of the sisterhood responding to the wave of new awareness and rebellion that was the 60's and 70's. She played a guitar and sang folk songs, for heaven's sake.

Danielle was stunned. It explained so much. It explained Mary's rush to embrace all of the things she had not chosen for so many years. It explained her complexity and her naiveté. But it was also an experience beyond Danielle's comprehension. Danielle felt she had to be very careful, that Mary was too innocent for her. Danielle felt sinful. It also made Danni want to live up to her rep, to be a little shocking, to show Mary sides of life she had never seen. Little did she know she would succeed beyond her wildest dreams. Little did she know Mary was part of her cure.

The moment of sharing passed, the tea glasses were again put away in the cupboard Danni's life continued but now Mary was not just a roommate, she was a project.

Carson had some special plans. He was very mysterious. Bring some warm clothes, he and Danni would be gone overnight he said. He picked her up after lunch. They drove for a long time. Bandit was with them. They drove way out in the desert; Danni had no idea where they were. Carson seemed to know exactly where he was, and where he was going.

They were going gradually up the side of hills and down the sides of hills, generally climbing towards higher ground in a landscape of hard yellow dirt and scruffy vegetation. It was a part of the desert Danni hadn't seen. Here the desert was a harsh, multi-breasted creature, the cleavages softer than the mounded crests. Carson kept sniffing; it was driving Danni crazy.

"Carson, what's wrong, do you have a cold, do you need a tissue?" She tried not to use the same tone she used with four-year-olds.

"I don't have a cold, my nose is all screwed up from snorting coke - it burns the tissues in your nose, they dry out. I had to stop doing coke because I kept getting nose bleeds."

"You did coke?" Danni tried not to sound as stunned as she felt or as naive. She thought of cocaine as hard drugs. She had tried a tiny bit once in her hippie days but she didn't know anyone who spoke so casually about it.

"God, I never thought about the possible side-effects. Why'd you do so much of it."

"I like it, I like the way it makes me feel."

"Where are we going anyway?" Danni didn't want to discuss cocaine anymore.

"It's a surprise."

But now Danni felt like she was headed out into the deserted desert with a stranger. She realized that she didn't really know Carson very well. She started to get paranoid. She started to fantasize about the possible dangers of her position. She started thinking about death again. Lately her fear made every new experience a potential giver of a violent end. Danni wanted to defend herself against sudden death and especially against pain by anticipating disaster before it happened. She played out each adventure to its worst possible outcome; she was assailed by all the sudden, numerous and painful ways death could come to such a fragile being as herself (or any person). Her fears grew out of the lines she cast into the future from each event in her life, which connected to a terrible pain-filled end.

When she went for a ride, in her mind she saw the crash at the side of the road. She saw the yellow and red lights of the rescue vehicles and the police. She saw the horror and avid interest on the faces of the spectators.

When she got into a plane she already saw the plane below her, scattered parts still smoking on the snowy ground below, this scene eerily quiet because no one knew they were there yet.

When she slept with a man she already saw her bruised and mutilated body discovered naked, twined among the sheets or half-covered with the fallen leaves, photographer's flashbulbs snapping. She saw the lurid picture on the front page of the newspaper.

A chill went up her spine. But she dismissed it. She felt guilty about her train of thought. She started to sing quietly with the music on the tape deck. Carson looked over at her with a smile.

"We're almost there."

Where, Danni thought?

They were at the nipple of one of the mounds. They were on a slim dirt track through a wilderness of small trees, cactus and scrub. Danni had just become aware of her surroundings again. She now saw that they were actually on a natural roller coaster, the downhill side of this particular mound, which they were perched precariously atop, was muddy with deep ruts, a concave thrill ride. Carson checked the four-wheel drive. Danni covered her eyes with her hands, but with the fingers spread so she could peek at her fate, she braced her feet on the dashboard. They went down, Carson guiding them safely and skillfully to the bottom. Danni breathed again.

"We're there," Carson said.

Danni sat up and looked around. They were in a deep canyon. There was a stream and lining its banks were cottonwood trees showing the silver backs of their leaves in a light breeze. Danni realized Carson had done this for her. She was touched by this effort.

"You remembered the cottonwood tree."

"I thought of this spot the minute you told me about the tree in your backyard. I love this spot."

"It's great Carson."

They got out of the truck, Bandit sniffing and running, changing directions, not sure which way to investigate first, but obviously happy to be free in these surroundings. They walked a ways down the stream under the cottonwoods. It was late in the day. The light was soft and diffuse through the leaves on the huge trees. The stream was small and danced along over mossy rocks. Danni breathed in the air which had momentarily lost its desert dryness and which had the lush, fuller, more vegetable scent of home. She wouldn't allow herself to feel homesick. She smiled at Carson. He held her hand for a bit as they walked along.

They eventually wandered back to the truck. Carson opened the tailgate and pulled the cooler closer. They sat on the tailgate popping tops off cold beers and eating sandwiches Carson had brought along. Bandit didn't beg, Danni was impressed. Carson pulled out a bone he had brought for him.

"What do you and Bandit hunt for," Danni asked.

"Oh jackrabbits, quail, deer, wild pig, just about anything it's legal to kill."

Danni had never been sure how she felt about hunting. She didn't quite see all animals as Bambi characters. Eating meat didn't turn her off because she just refused to think too realistically about what she was eating. But she always felt a little prehistoric when she tackled a steak. She pictured the cave, the firelight flickering on the walls and the stick with the roasting meat, juices crackling. She pictured herself holding the meat in her hand as she sat on her haunches, juices running down her chin, dropping into the dirt at her feet. The hunter, her man, had returned tired from the hunt, his arrows frayed, a deer across his shoulders, smaller game hanging on a rawhide line she had made for him, slung over his left shoulder swinging in the space between his body and his arm. The dog lay with his whole body flattened out and relaxed between his bent hind legs and his stretched out forepaws, snout on the ground between the forepaws, eyes drowsily watching the cooking meat, the two people; sighs occasionally escaping.

"I'll take you hunting with me sometime," Carson said. The ochre walls of the cave retreated. Danni was back in the cottonwoods.

"OK," Danni answered feebly, not sure that she wanted to be in on the kill. Although she ate meat, she didn't see it killed. Danni scooped up spiders on a piece of paper and put them outside rather than kill them. Still it seemed hypocritical to eat meat and not actually admit that someone had to kill it.

"Is Bandit a good hunter?" Danni asked Carson, assuming she already knew the answer.

"Bandit was a great hunter, but he's getting old. He'll have to be put to sleep soon."

Danni was shocked. "Why? You mean he doesn't get put out to pasture, that's the thanks he gets, when he's no longer useful he just gets tossed aside."

One minute Danni felt she understood this man's simple needs, the next minute he seemed such a cold bastard, with no emotional attachment to anything or anybody. She could not understand him. It seemed he lived by different rules.

It was getting dark. They closed up the cooler and pushed it to the front of the truck bed.

"We better get the bedding from inside and make up the bed while we can still see," Carson said.

They climbed in the cab. Danni started pulling sleeping bags from behind the seat. Carson reached under the front seat and pulled out a flat wooden box with a latch. Danni, curious, watched out of the corner of her eye. She couldn't believe it. When he opened the box inside was a gun. A big mean looking pistol (six gun) sitting in a bed of green velveteen. Carson handled it lovingly. Danni broke out in a cold sweat. They would never find her body here in a shallow grave beside the cottonwoods. She would just disappear forever. What was she doing out her in the middle of the night? There was no one around, no one would know.

Carson put the gun back and tucked the box back under the seat.

"Com'on Danni, let's get this stuff organized," Carson said.

Danni sat still for a minute looking straight ahead, then she took a deep cleansing breath, shuddered involuntarily and said, "OK, Carson."

They were very cozy tucked into all the blankets with the chill night desert cottonwood air outside, doomed Bandit curled up between their legs. Carson apparently knew nothing of Danni's inner fears. Surprisingly Danni slept deeply and securely cuddled by Carson and Bandit, under the magnificent desert stars in the bed of the red Ford truck.

11
Tucson

Danielle was reading <u>Garp</u>. She was propped up in her double bed with sunlight squeezing around the edges of the closed blinds. That was the only problem with this perpetual sunshine. It was difficult to find a properly gloomy, drizzly, clammy day to accommodate any vague spiritual depression that might arise. That state of wanting to abdicate responsibilities and just sleep in, to shut out the clamor of people and events, to snuggle into a cocoon of blankets and pillows, must be a basically northern phenomenon, Danni thought. Hard to cocoon when a sheet would suffice for covering, when merry droplets of golden light illuminated lazy strata of tiny dust particles in delicate bars across your bed. But Danni was feeling slightly depressed. She had been thinking; that always got her in trouble, especially without A. A., or Nicole or Amanda around to present more positive interpretations. Danni was distressed because things were going well. Now when life seemed good Danni planned for disaster. She didn't want to be caught unawares. She had cataloged the flaws that would ruin Perez, end her relationship with Carson, and bring disgrace in her graduate studies.

She was reading to escape her thoughts, her mood, to arise once again to float among the dust motes on the cheerful particles of yellow light. Garp had just learned that his wife was having an affair with a student. Here it was plain and simple, the unexpected disaster. Garp, enjoying his family, believing in their blissful union, suddenly realizes his wife has not been tuned in. He's VHF, she's UHF, he's AM, she's FM. She agrees to break off her relationship, Garp grieved and angry takes his children to the movies.

He's restless, he's heart sore, he can't watch the movie. They head home through the blinding rain (he can't cry, but at least the sky has the decency to help him out). Wife is in the driveway, in the student's car, giving a last farewell gift to her young lover at his insistence. Garp loves to turn off his lights, throw the car into neutral and coast downhill into his driveway. Danni already can see the divine justice in the outcome (she thinks). She's laughing, she's hooting as teeth decapitate essential flesh. But she hasn't foreseen the retribution. "The sins of the [mothers]" -- she hasn't foreseen the awful price of the faithless, libidinal indulgence of Mrs. Garp and the insensible complacency of Garp. Danni finds tears of laughter metamorphosed instantly to tears of grief, hoots of righteous mirth turned to expletives of disbelief, cries of "foul," "unfair". Divine justice becomes cosmic paradox. Why should one child die and one child lose an eye on the naked shift bar? It's too much. What was already painful is now gaping wound? No dainty scars here, they were slashed from chest to groin, truly heroic scars, never to disappear under hair regrowth or makeup.

What a writer! Danielle is uplifted, pulled out of her doomy reveries, out of her bed, out to tell Mary "you must read this book, it's so amazing." She can't communicate the why, she would have to use words and she wants to just pass on the consciousness, she needs telepathy. But she's up, out of the chrysalis; rain clouds no longer necessary. Because of John Irving, Danni can again get on with her life.

Mary and Danielle knock around the house in shorts, Danni studying sometimes in the living room, sometimes in her bedroom. Mary studies at the kitchen table. They're immersed, for each the other doesn't exist, except on an occasional sun tea break. This will go on for days, Danni knows, until exams are over. They look like twins. They are sexless, they wear no make up, their hair is unstyled, tucked up or back. They run their hands through the shorter hair in front. It stands up in greasy Medusa whorls around their faces. It's not a pretty sight.

They carry their books everywhere, the books like growths, a new limb, a new breast. They carry them from room to room, to the library, to classes, even to the pool. They live in a haze of smoke (even Mary borrows a cigarette now and then), coffee, tea, words and the thoughts of others. Pages of notes rest everywhere. The tasteless furniture is refinished in college rule and blue ink.

Danielle and Mary, when reality starts to slip, take longer breaks. They go to visit the couple next door, Bev and Russ. They're a young Air Force couple with a very happy, very bald baby girl, Tina. They have no exams to pass, no grand designs to distract their attention. They live a normal life, watching TV, listening to their stereo, seeing friends, swimming in the pool. Their life is lived for pleasure, for fun. They are always stoned. To Danni and Mary, they seem pointless, and shallow, and enviable. They are earthbound and seemingly centered and just being with them obliterates weightlessness, recalls the law of gravity.

Or, they visit Amy and Ann, two doors down the other way. Young single girls with jobs: for Danni they are her past, for Mary they are Exhibit B (Danni being Exhibit A) and her longed for future. They have jobs, they are secretaries, and they have boyfriends, big boyfriends on "I mean business" motorcycles with beards and neckbands. These guys are not "Hell's Angels." Their jeans are clean and new, they wear clean black polo shirts with little stand-up collars. They all sit in Amy and Ann's living room, Mary and Danni included, legs spread, beers resting on a knee. Or they move their chairs out onto the sidewalk in front of the apartment and hide behind the jasmine. They take turns conversing; they keep their remarks short. Although there may be weighty issues, they are not discussed when Danni and Mary are around.

Sometimes Tim, the teenager from down court comes to visit. They love it when he drops by because he flirts harmlessly and constantly, driven by the sexual drive of late puberty. They comb their fingers through their tortured tresses before they let him in. His juices are flowing. His chemicals diffuse from his fine young pores into the air around him. Danni and Mary become animated, their faces light, their smiles flash. He always sits in the armchair by the front window. Danni sits on the couch, Mary in the sling chair. Their bodies bend towards him, an elbow on each knee, chin resting on open palms. They are helpless victims of an invisible chemotropic invasion. He feels powerful, he always comes back. When he leaves, Danni and Mary retreat again to their separate domains, the color leaves their cheeks. Gradually they shift gears from id to superego, carpe diem to puritan ethic, woman to neuter. The pens scratch across the pages, the new sheets are added to the others, voices whisper arcane lists of names and theories intended to capitalize on the curiosity of toddlers, to set them off on a path that will lead to their assimilation of 5,000 years of cultural memory.

When Danielle, in the midst of this academic miasma, found herself behind the desk at Sonora Safari, she felt that her senses were cobwebby, sluggish. She was not at all prepared for Perez. The jerky motions of his skinny legs and arms, the muscles around his mouth and eyes as his smile came and went, seemed, from a purely intellectual view, to be the motions of a loose-jointed wooden puppet acting out some bizarre excitable state. As Danni's emotional rheostat gradually restored balance, cold intellect diminished, specimen dissolved slowly into human, into the Perez Danni knew and loved. Perez was high again, he was up, he couldn't hold still, he was dancing in place. Fred was there too. There was a tour today. He sat at his desk opposite Danni, implacable and stolid, seemingly unaffected while Perez's future business plans blew from his lips like iridescent bubbles. He wanted Danni to get this supplier and that supplier. He wanted a big shipment of desert camping gear, a shipment of footgear. There were T-shirts to be ordered. He issued his commands with total surety and then faced Danni with humble questions in his eyes. "What do you think, is this the right thing to do?" "Did I speak to that company like a businessman?" "Did I earn his respect?"

Danni looked the questions right back at him. She didn't think the orders were a good idea at all. They were overstocked; he was buying on consignment when he had cash. But facing Perez was like facing a small, proud boy with an inept science fair project. She couldn't disapprove. Her smile, her willingness to help, made her an accomplice in entrepreneurial suicide; belied her doubts and dissension. The companies did not want to send the merchandise. There was the matter of the previous unpaid shipment. Perez loved a challenge; he had no doubts now. He knew his powers of persuasion. A check was in the mail. Release the new shipment as soon as they received partial payment for the old. Business was good. No problem. They all agreed the shipments would arrive.

Danni, who could not say no in person, had at least believed sanity would reign in direct proportion with the distance from the whirlwind. What she hadn't factored in is that these salesmen did not essentially care whether Perez succeeded or did not. They would either get their money or their merchandise.

Perez subsided after this burst of frantic administrative creativity. He puttered around in the shop, talking to customers at the counter about the rigors of the desert and the accessories of hunters. Customers stayed longer when Perez was behind the counter. He made coffee. He talked with Fred about the tour and helped him pack the jeep. He looked over Danni's shoulder as she filled the columns in the account book. Finally he sat at Danni's desk behind the table where she was keeping the books. Jake wandered in. Danielle retreated further into the books. She still thought he was a sleaze bucket, just waiting around to grab leftovers. But she couldn't resist eavesdropping on their conversation.

"You seen Chet lately?" Jake asked.

"Yeah man, he was around last Saturday. Him and Ginger are havin' a party in a couple of weeks. You goin'?"

"Sure, they told me 'bout it coupla weeks ago. Riley's gonna be there." Jake said.

That low life and his one-upmanship, Danni thought. He probably hung around until they had to invite him. Danni wondered who Riley was.

"You and Gina seem pretty tight lately, man?"

"She's been a real bitch, though," Perez said quietly, " she don't wanta go nowhere, man. She threw some dishes at me the other night. I had ta get outta there fast. I stayed away two whole days. She's a little better since I been back there."

"Why don't you dump her, man, find a new woman? You need a more peaceful old lady."

Danni shuddered. She didn't think Perez had a healthy relationship but she also didn't want him on the loose. Although he was sometimes flirtatious it was just for fun, their relationship was business only. Much as she loved him, Danni liked things this way. She sure didn't want his eyes turning her way. She sent up a silent prayer that Gina and Perez would continue their neurotic tango, or that, at least, another woman would catch Perez' eye.

"You got any cigarettes, man? I'm out of smokes," Jake whined.

What a dog, Danni thought. This was what she loved about this place. It brought out the worst in her. It was her National Enquirer self, the perfect paradoxical companion to her collegiate alter ego.

"Well, I gotta go. Have a good one," Jake said as he slinked out the door, Perez' cigarette hanging from his bottom lip.

Danni cringed. Forever after she automatically distrusted anyone who said "have a good one."

"Danni, you almost done with those books, they have to be at the accountant's place by 4:30?" Perez asked.

"I'm on the last day now, " Danni said as she wrote.

"I'll give you the address. You take it over there and drop it off on your way home. You live over north, right."

"O.K., Perez, no problem." But Danielle was a little annoyed. She didn't want all these responsibilities. In case something went wrong she wanted to be well out of it. A cloud of impending doom hung over Perez's tangled electric head, perhaps visible only to her. She wasn't willing to go down with his ship. She packed up the books, got the directions to the accountant's office, and went home to those other books, the textbooks.

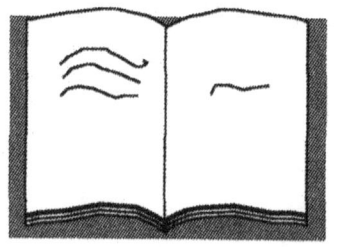 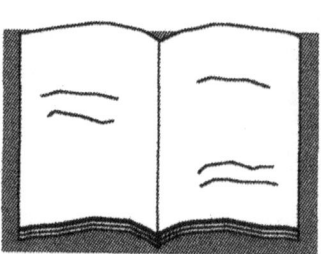

12
Tucson

Danielle had taken all her exams; she had one paper left to do. It was due next week. The research was all done; the rough draft was finished. Now she just had to edit and type it. Kate's party was Sunday. Danni was going but she was nervous about it. She had seen Carson several times during exams. They really didn't go anywhere anymore. Danni usually went to his house, he cooked dinner, they watched TV and went to bed. The intoxication had obviously worn off. Danni was starting to see a certain coolness about Carson, he was warning her not to get too involved. And he was so lazy. There was the matter of the bathroom. Also he had borrowed a horse which he kept in the backyard. The function of the horse was to keep the tough old desert grass trimmed so Carson wouldn't have to cut it.

Danni rarely spent the night. She liked to be home in the morning. She would leave at 3 or 4 a. m. and drive home through the quiet streets. She loved Tucson then. The air was cool, the darkness back lit and luminous. The melancholy guilt-ridden wistfulness of the illicit post coital state would ride with her. She was weary of this male-female dynamic which she thought she would escape each time a new relationship began but which reappeared each time, redundant and symbolic. On the way home she would sing to herself and to the night.

"Mammas, don't let your babies grow up to be cowboys. They're always alone and they're never at home, even with someone they love."

That might explain Carson's intimacy problems, but it didn't explain hers. She thought a lot as she crept home during those early morning hours. "What did she want from him anyway?" "What would it be like to be married to him?"

"Don't ask for what you don't want because you might get it." But she still didn't want to be rejected again.

Finally Danielle accepted that Carson was not going to ask her to the party. She could either ignore the situation or confront it. She dreaded confrontation. Her voice always betrayed her. She meant to sound confident, and justifiably angry. She usually sounded wimpy and wounded. Instead of turning rejection into victory the outcome generally resembled more closely "the agony of defeat." But now that she was back in life, she couldn't opt out again. What was it they used to say, "you're either on the bus, or off the bus"? Deep. Simple.

"Carson," she began tentatively, "are you going to Kate's party?"

"I was thinking about it, why?"

(Was there an edge in his voice?) Immediately Danni felt defensive. "I'm going too. Why aren't we going together?" Danni got it out.

"I want to go by myself," Carson said, "we're not a couple. I'm usually a loner. I just want to hang loose."

Danni knew that one of her main problems in a relationship was that she could always understand the feelings of her partner, or so she thought. She didn't want to discount those feelings (what about her own?). She rationalized everything. After all she was a 'liberated' female (at least she tried to be). She believed in the rights of the individual (which individual?). And she certainly didn't want to have to force someone to love her; either they did, or they didn't (although how could any man not love someone so ultimately lovable?) Danni lived by her own self-esteem dialectic. She was wonderful, unique, and creative; she was ugly, dull and unlovable. Will the real Danni Giroux please stand up? They were both real. One represented the way she felt when she was alone. The other the way she felt in public. Oh no, she really was back in life.

She didn't get angry, she didn't leave in a huff. Her deep-seated insecurities would not allow her to take a stand. She'd go to the party alone. She would prove that she wasn't a clinging female.

At first it worked. Kate's backyard was huge, with a stone patio and a brick fireplace. There was no grass, but the tough dusty-green weeds had been mowed to resemble a meadow. The rancho, as she remembered it, was tucked in at the base of the same mountains Danni drove towards every day as she returned to her apartment. The mountains seemed enormous and close but they were probably still too distant to walk to. They were purple, they were cobalt blue, and they dominated the landscape. Danni couldn't get enough of them. Again she noticed how they turned all the foliage slightly blue, the way a blue spruce is blue. For a while Danni was lulled by the beauty.

Pretty soon she was surrounded by groups of unfamiliar laughing, drinking, talking people. She roused herself from her reverie to socialize. Carson wasn't there yet. She sat on the patio talking with some of Kate's friends, mostly women. The men were in a clump by the keg, near the barbecue pit. These were nice women; they talked about child rearing and decorating and their jobs. Danielle was enjoying herself. Then Carson arrived. She tried not to, but out of the corner of her eyes she watched him, followed his progress. First stop, the keg, men-talk, locker room laughter. He joined the volley ball game that was starting up. That's where the young women were with their short shorts and bikini tops. He was all over the 'court.' What a helpful guy! It was starting to bother her that he hadn't said hi. Kate called to her to join the volley ball game. She played on Carson's side of the net. Still, he didn't acknowledge her. No one would ever have known they were acquainted, let alone intimate. Danni smiled in his direction, still nothing, a flicker. She left the game. Someone took her place immediately. Apparently her departure wasn't worth noticing. She wandered back to the patio to try to regain the rapport she had felt before Carson came but she was agitated. She couldn't enjoy anyone. She was angry and hurt. And there was that paper waiting at home to be typed.

Danielle decided to go home. She said goodbye to Kate and drove off in the blue isolation booth. She drove home with tears rolling down her face. Well at least she could cry. That was progress. It didn't take long and there she was back in front of the typewriter with a slight buzz on and a heavy sadness in her heart, the martyr to professordom. The phone rang. Mary wasn't home. On the fifth ring Danni decided to answer. It really was Carson.

"What's wrong with you?" he said.

Unbelievable, Danni thought.

"Carson, you didn't even say hi, you acted as if you didn't know me. I felt invisible."

"I would have gotten around to it, I told you how it would be," said heartless, the desperado.

"Well, I can't deal with that" (it was ultimatum time). "Either we're together or we aren't."

"Danni, I want it casual, no strings," said Cowboy Bob.

"No way," said Danni. (Don't ask for what you don't want because you might get it, her brain repeated.) But she didn't. He was happy to let her go. Ultimatums brought fire to the eyes of the Gringo Kid.

"Well, I guess that's goodbye." The shoot out at the OK Corral was over. One combatant walked away the victor. It wasn't Danni (or was it?) Now Danni was a free agent again. Freedom and loneliness are directly proportional. She seemed heir to plenty of both.

Danni hung up the phone. She obviously knew nothing about men, but she knew how to write a paper. At first she banged away halfheartedly at the typewriter. Her heart had on cement overshoes. Gradually the task at hand consumed her attention and while her heart did not exactly soar, she was too busy to notice.

Once Danielle turned the paper in she was finished with the spring semester. Summer classes didn't start for another week so Danni planned to put in more hours at Sonora Safari. Lily was coming in August and they were going to the Grand Canyon and Las Vegas, so she needed the money.

The big desert bash was all over at Sonora Safari. It was a big success. Sales were good. It was too hot for many tours right now but they were doing a really good walk-in business. Gina and Perez were not doing well, however. Every time Danni saw them, which fortunately wasn't often, they were either sullen or locked in mortal combat. It was a sick relationship, but neither sufferer seemed able to chose health. Perez told Gina he would kill himself if she left. He said it frequently and in front of anyone who happened to be present. Knowing Perez, Gina believed him.

Perez hardly came to S.S. and D.T. at all these days. When he did he stayed for five minutes, took all the cash from the drawer and split. He was high one time, low the next. His activity level was frenetic and his thoughts were unfocused. One time Danielle thought she noticed needle marks on his arm. Everyone asked for him, but he was rarely around when they came. The heart and soul was leaking out of the business. Danni kept things going as best she could. She waited on customers; she took inventory, kept the books, made deposits in the bank and talked the creditors on the phone. But it was "doom in June" as Perez two-stepped out the door with all the cash receipts. Danni could see the handwriting in the books and it was red. Unless Perez came to his senses soon it would be Sonora Safari and Disaster Tours. Danni tried to discuss things with Fred but he didn't care. He was happy that there were no tours. He was on vacation. As long as his check was there when he came to get it everything was fine with him.

Jake stopped by three times, which was about three times too many, but he never caught up with Perez. At least he had the decency to be worried. Frank and Sylvia stopped in.

They were just back from San Diego with their upper class selves. They were scandalized by San Diego morality. Apparently the people in their trailer park had exhibited some bizarre sexual behaviors. Danni was a little surprised to learn they minded. But they were nice people and they too were concerned about Perez. Regular customers asked at the counter or over the phone for Perez time after time and always hung up disappointed. Danielle thought again about getting out while the proverbial getting was good, but something held her there paralyzed, waiting to see how things would come out. After all, there's no way off a roller coaster until the ride is over.

13
Tucson

If spring in Tucson is hot, summer in Tucson bakes. Danni arrived everywhere soaking wet. The little blue Toyota bakery had no air-conditioning; it had snow tires and a rear window defroster. Her rust proofing warranty was wearing out. That oriental cutie was a hot box on wheels. Danni burned coil patterns on the backs of her legs from the sun-baked metal coils inside her air cushion. She looked like a waffle.

Danielle perspired (it was more like evapotranspired) her way to classes, to Sonora Safari, to the health spa (she must be too fat, after all she was a reject), to the beauty parlor and shopping. Luckily her wet clothing dried out as soon as she stepped out of the car. She ate lunch at the school cafeteria because it was air-conditioned. She left notes for Perez to get a swamp cooler for Sonora Safari. She stayed in her apartment and ate Middle Eastern food. She ate Mexican food. She drank margaritas. It was so hot the bottoms snapped right off her tall ice tea glasses. She saved them to show at the department store when she got home.

In Syracuse Danielle stayed inside in the winter, here she wanted to stay in all summer. But Kate lured her out. She took her places that were so hot her brains felt addled. You couldn't think in this heat, after a while you just gave into it, duh. Kate took her to Old Tucson for the shoot out. They went to the Desert Museum (it looked like a zoo to Danni, except the plants had names too.) She read the epitaph for George, the Mountain Lion. They went to the Mission. Danni liked them all as much as she could under this brutal desert sun. Kate even took her to Green Valley to a small farm where they could pick their own vegetables. It was cooler there. They had yellow watermelons.

At night, now that Danni was unattached, she went out with the "girls" to the bars. They went to *The Bum Steer* where there were all kinds of Western antiques hanging from the walls and ceilings. The guys there had horseshoe tournaments in the alley. They went to *the Loft*; they went to hotel discos. They were wild women on the town. Danni even tried to learn the country swing, but she still danced better if she could do it without touching. Mary, the innocent lamb, went with them on these jaunts. She had more fun than any of them. It was all new to her.

They also were cultural during that endless summer. They went to the *Tucson Art Museum*. They went shopping at *La Placida Village*. They went to the Greek restaurant and to a Shakespeare play in the courtyard at the *Tucson Civic Center Plaza*. Danni even met a new man, Cambridge Mercedes, a cute little banker with tight blond curls (bleached?). He lasted for two dates. After a struggle in his truck bed at the drive-in Danni decided so much for ambitious preppy guys. Cowboys were at least polite and even maybe romantic in their own way. She heard Carson was seeing a young beauty named Colleen. He was head over heels. He wanted to marry her. But she supposedly wasn't ready. Danni didn't see him at all. Their paths never crossed.

Mary's education in depravity continued. One night she picked up two guys at a bar, one for Danielle, one for her. The guys invited them back to their hotel room. Danni tried to see if Mary had any idea what that meant but Mary obviously took them at their word. They visited for a few minutes, had one drink, toured the courtyard swimming pool and left two speechless guys gaping as they made their escape. Danni would have liked to think that Mary was a damned good strategist, but it was probably more like dumb luck.

Danni had eventually been invited to Chet and Ginger's party. Chet came in to Sonora Safari one day and invited her. Chet was the only one who saw Perez. For some reason whenever Chet showed up, Perez did too. Very curious,

Danni thought. That Chet was a handsome man, even a polite man, but Danni still believed, not a nice one.

"Bring someone," Chet said.

He probably meant a man, but there wasn't one, so Danielle took Mary. As soon as they walked in the door Danni was sorry. Danni knew these people did drugs. You could tell by the way the apartment looked. It was furnished from the Salvation Army. It wasn't dirty. Ginger obviously still had a grip on reality, but it looked like every hippie pad Danni had ever seen or lived in. The music was hard rock and it was deafening. Danni didn't recognize the artist, but she recognized the state of mind. Someone handed them beers. Danni was ready to leave five minutes after she walked in but Mary wanted to stay. Here was Life with a capital L, the seamy, steamy side. Mary wouldn't miss it for the world. It was a sociological study. So Danni sat on a cushion on the floor.

Jake stopped by.

"Hi Danni, gotta cigarette." Danni read his lips.

She gave him one.

"Gotta light?" It hadn't taken much imagination to figure that one out.

Danni lit his cigarette. "Maybe you'd like me to smoke it for you too," she thought.

"I saw Perez," Jake yelled, "he said he couldn't make it tonight. Him and Gina had a blow out so he's got to make things up to her."

Probably Gina told him she absolutely wasn't coming, Danni thought.

"How'd he seem to you?" Danni asked, during a rare musical lull.

"Geez, I don't know, he was pretty down when I saw him."

Then Mary came over. Danielle introduced her to Jake. Jake said hello and slithered off elsewhere. That Mary was a real peach.

Ginger drifted by and met Mary. She was the hostess, just checking up on her guests. Did they need another beer? They didn't. Danni didn't see Chet although she heard his calm baritone every so often from the back of the apartment.

"Danni, I have to go to the bathroom," Mary said, "come with me."

There was hardly anyone in the living room. Danni knew the bathroom, kitchen, etc. must be at the back of the house, because all the noise was coming from that direction. She really didn't want to go back there but she didn't dare send Mary alone. So she unscrambled her legs from the cushion, picked up her purse and they headed off.

Danielle's worst fears were confirmed as they passed the first bedroom on the way to the bathroom. There were several people in there. Danni could see the lines of coke neatly arranged on the big mirror that was lying flat on top of the tall dresser. They were using straws to snort the stuff. Inhale, ah. They were oblivious. They didn't even bother to close the door. Danni knew they had invited, Riley. She had also found out that he was the other partner, the cop. Judging by what she was seeing, Danni could only assume that he moonlighted as a druggie, or that he had declined the invitation. She knew what he looked like. She didn't see him anywhere at the party. She had seen him one day when he finally wandered into the shop looking for Perez. When Perez wasn't there, he introduced himself and asked Danni to leave Perez a message. He looked like Clark Kent. Danielle had thought that all he needed was a phone booth. He certainly didn't look like the type to do drugs, he looked very straight. They must have known he wouldn't come to the party.

"What are they doing, Danni?" Mary asked her in a low voice, but by no means a whisper.

"Sh-h-h, I'll tell you later," Danni said. "Go to the bathroom, then we're leaving."

While Mary was in the bathroom Danni went to find their hostess.

"I have to leave Ginger. It was really nice of you to invite me."

"You have to go already?"

"Yes I have some papers to finish," Danni said lamely. "You know college students, always studying."

"I understand," said Ginger, who probably had had at least a couple of years of college and who probably knew it was just an excuse.

Danni didn't think Ginger really minded though. She was preoccupied with putting together some snacks and talking with some woman who was obviously a good friend.

"I'll talk to you," Ginger said, "maybe we can go shopping sometime."

"O.K., give me a call," Danni answered as she grabbed Mary by the hand and pulled her along toward the door. "Bye!"

Then they were out, into the fresh night air, into the patient blue buggy, off to stability, sanity and the straight life. Mary's education had taken a giant step forward.

14

Tucson

The summer session went very quickly. Danielle only took two courses but they met every day. She was in school until one; she went to Sonora Safari until 4 p.m. Then she went home and did assignments until "I'd rather be in Tucson" time or beyond. Except for her treks with Kate as a sightseer or her transformation into her alter ego as a single "swinger", Danni lived the life of a dedicated, hardworking academic, "early to bed, early to rise."

By the time Lily arrived for her two weeks vacation, which was actually ten days due to the contortions airlines force on Super Savers, Danni was finished with her last paper, project, exam, and was so completely bummed out by Perez that she couldn't wait to get out of there. Perez was closing up shop for two weeks to go on vacation (from what?)

Lily was her same sensible self and Danni was incredibly glad to see her, someone from home, same parents, same memories. Danni hadn't felt homesick lately but it all came flooding in. She called her mother and Lily got on the extension and they all had a good long talk.

They stayed in Tucson for three days. Danni took Lily to the Mission, to the Desert Museum and to Old Tucson. It was fun to be the tour guide instead of the touree. But it was still brutally hot. Lily wasn't used to it. She made Danni feel like a veteran. Lily complained, she bought hats, they bought lemonade. Danni showed her El Parador, the Mexican place in the brick courtyard with all the plants. She taught her the spicy-Mexican-food-followed-by-pitchers-of-margaritas trick. Lily liked it. Danni had discovered chili rellenos so she ordered them everywhere she went. Only a few places made them the way Danni liked them with the fresh green chili peppers stuffed with a mild cheese and deep fried in a delicate batter. Lily was a picky eater; she had no guts when it came to food. She had cheese enchiladas because they didn't put any of that guacamole or other crap on them as Lily explained. But margaritas were right up her alley.

They spent a day at the Colossal Caves but when it came to the moment of decision Danni couldn't go down inside. Lily mocked her, but Danni knew she'd want to get out of there as soon as she got in. Lily wouldn't go without her. They drove back to Tucson with Lily's anger and disappointment. Being a chicken also has social drawbacks.

The next day, still hardly speaking they left for the Grand Canyon. Lily had made their reservations months ago. Gradually the uplift in spirits that comes with setting out on the road eased the tension between them and they talked of the past as they drove along. They rehashed all the old Michael stuff. Lily had never liked him anyway. Danni, however, still couldn't accept that he was all bad.

"What do you mean? He was a sleaze --!" Lily said.

"He never made any promises, never pretended to be more than just a friend," Danni defended.

"Geez Louise, he was there every night, from after work until bed time. He watched TV. I couldn't get away from the guy," Lily argued.

"He helped cook the dinners," Danni said weakly. "He was a great cook," she added, trying to change the subject.

But Lily, the lover of plain food, was not distracted into reminiscences of gourmet delights. She could see past the Veal Oscar.

"He acted like he was courting you, he knew you were falling for him and he liked it. And I think he really enjoyed making a fool out of you at the end. Danni, you couldn't eat after that, you still don't eat right."

"Thanks a lot," Danni said.

The sisters were off and running again. Good friends and sisters cannot travel together without arguing. Danni wasn't sure why but it seemed to be a law of the universe. Eventually they were at Phoenix and the rigors of navigation ended the conversation and restored peace once again.

"Kate said to look for Red Rocks, Sedona," Danni said. "She said it's too beautiful to miss. I hope we get to see it."

Lily consulted the map. She was the current navigator.

"It's pretty far still, Lily said and it's not on this route. We would have to take a slight detour."

"Well, I vote yes," Danni said.

Lily thought they should get to the Grand Canyon as early as possible but then she capitulated. All right, they could go and just look and then get back on the road. So they went. They could see the red rocks from far away. They thought at first that the sun was playing tricks on them, but as they got closer, they could see the strong red-orange, layer after layer in varying degrees of intensity, laid down centuries ago in the sandstone under some long lost inland sea. Now worn by weather and time these earthy sentinels stood in narrow splendor above the less colorful layers of underlying rock, mighty red cliffs. They stopped the car and took a whole roll of pictures, but later, when they were developed, they didn't show the dazzling brilliance of those red rocks. They looked dark and dull. But the camera in their minds had a more precise mechanism, apparently. Their minds remembered those colors in all their glory.

They didn't stay long, they didn't go to the chapel that they saw way up on top of one of the red cliffs, but they were awed by the magnificence and Danni didn't have to listen to any lectures about useless side trips. Sights like this made all the squabbling travelers do melt away, this was what people traveled for, Danni thought.

The road climbed after Red Rocks. It was gradual but continual for mile after mile. By the time they arrived at Flagstaff they were in a totally different climate. They had left the desert behind. You could tell it got cold here. You could tell they had a real winter with snow and everything.

There were pine forests with the rich needle loam underneath, with the sunlight slanting through upraised boughs, streams of softened sunlight traveling down in wide mote-filled beams that dissipated before they could reach the forest floor. This was familiar; this could have been the Adirondacks. And that was pretty much the climate they found at the Grand Canyon. Apparently, at the bottom of the canyon hot desert conditions prevailed, but up here at the south rim it was pine forest. The architectural design of all the buildings blended with the vegetation. Hotels and motels had been fashioned from slabs of barked wood cut in inch-thick boards. They were stained dark brown and looked solid, commodious and brooding, in concert with the tall pines around them. The motel where Lily and Danni had reservations was not one of the big impressive ones overlooking the canyon. There were no massive stone walls around their motel or flagstone patios as there were on the big hotels. It was just a line of rooms set back on the non-canyon side of the road, several miles away from the action.

There were all kinds of things to do, mule packing down into the canyon, horseback riding along the rim, hiking expeditions to the land of the Havasupai where there was a gorgeous natural pool with a water fall. There were also airplane and helicopter flights into or over the canyon. Danni and Lily wanted to do it all but they found that people had booked expeditions a year in advance. They probably would not have passed the physical required of hikers anyway. They couldn't even go horse back riding which Lily wanted to do badly. So they stood on the edge in various spots with all of the other tourists, almost none of whom spoke English. They took photos and marveled at what a river and internal tectonic forces could do, but in the end they had to admit that it was just a big hole in the ground, great to see, but boring to stare at for hour after hour. They got a lot more enjoyment from watching the Japanese, French and Scandinavian tourists and the chipmunks and squirrels than from the canyon itself. They couldn't even get seats in the good restaurant because it was full. Sometimes things you do on the spur of the moment turn out better than things you plan. Anyway, they were leaving for Las Vegas in the morning. They added up the mileage on the map and figured it would take them about three hours.

They added wrong. It took seven hours through a landscape of badlands, red and black bare rock looking like it had poured out of a volcano and hardened there in shining runnels and ridges. It was hot, hotter than a traffic jam in Tucson. If Tucson was God's oven, this land was God's furnace. They were unprepared for it. They had nothing to drink in this blue metal Hades. They felt flushed and their heads ached dully. There were no quaint little gas stations with soda machines along the way. There was nothing but this vast wasteland. Lily and Danni marveled at the size of it. When they finally rounded the last high bend and saw the Hoover Dam holding back the shining water; when they saw the boats and the water skiers, it looked like a mirage. They understood why the Native Americans called it "the water of life". Danni didn't even care that they were headed down the steepest incline on the sheer face of one of the steepest cliffs she had ever seen. They were through the badlands. But they were not through the desert. The watery interlude was very short. However, they did find a gas station and a soda machine. If they had realized what they looked like they would have found a mirror.

Lily had harbored a fantasy, she told Danni, ever since she booked their reservations at the hotel, that they would sweep up to the big glass front door and be smothered in valets and red caps like putting on a mink coat. These uniformed gallants would whisk their luggage out of their hands, actually would fight over who would get to do the whisking. Danni and Lily would be treated like royalty. After all this was a renowned hotel.

However, Lily had not foreseen that they would arrive looking like prospectors, faces covered with gray dust over a bright pink heat flush. She had not foreseen that the hotel service staff would be on strike. As the blue metal dust bucket drove up to the glass doors under the portico, a hotel employee came forward to the window on the passenger side.

"Drive your car to that parking lot over there," he said, pointing to the right of the building, "and then carry your bags back here to the door."

If they hadn't just come out of the mouth of hell they might have thought to leave their bags at the famous portico and then park the car. But they had and so they didn't. They dutifully drove to the parking lot where they had to park at the far end. They limped back to the grand entrance, bags banging against knees and rear ends. They had to stop several times to rest. They crept in, finally, through the glass doors which were looking less grand by now. They waited in line to check in, gazing around them in wonder like the pair of hicks they almost were. Lily would have to wait a while longer for the royal treatment.

The casino was the lobby and it was enormous, it made the check-in counter look like an afterthought. Danni stared at the Keno room. It looked like a disco classroom. It had rows of seats all facing a board where electronic numbers flashed. She had always suspected that she was a potential gambling addict, only waiting for that first exposure to be hooked forever. Danielle had always liked lotteries and raffles and Bingo, to the embarrassment of all her educated friends. It was also clear to Danni that however much the possibility of instant wealth attracted her, she was not a winner. She had never won at anything. She never even won one of the eighth prize AM/FM radios in the *Publisher's Clearinghouse Sweepstakes*. Danni had once almost won one hundred dollars at Bingo but by the time she noticed that she hadn't covered one of the called numbers, three other people also had Bingo, so she only got twenty-five dollars. In spite of this Danni felt a powerful pull right now towards the slot machines. Lily had to use her best logic and finally physical force to get her to go up to the room first in order to leave off the bags. They had to carry their own bags to their room, of course, because there were not enough management people to replace all the service workers.

Once Danni was away from the plush, gaudy and glittering lobby the pull of the slots calmed itself. They were in the new wing. It was a nice room and it was made up. Lily was slightly mollified. Danni had by now consulted a mirror so she was horrified. If she had gone to the slot machines looking like this she would have truly been headed for the depths of degradation. It took a long time for both of them to repair the ravages of the wasteland.

Lily pointed out to Danni as they applied fresh makeup that she, Danni, only had forty dollars.

"Actually, since we want to go to a show and we have to eat for two days, Danni, you really can't afford to gamble at all," Lily said.

" Come to Las Vegas and not gamble -- ?" said Danni aghast.

"Hand over the money, Danni," Lily said, "I'll hold on to it for you. You can have ten dollars for the slots, that's it."

That sounded O.K. to Danni, who had no idea how fast money could disappear into a slot machine.

"I'm ready, let's go," Danni said.

Lily, who could see the dollar signs in Danni's eyes, and the lint in her change purse, said, "Danni, let's not waste the daylight in a dark casino, let's put on our bathing suits and go out by the pool."

"There's a pool here?" Danni said, "O.K., I'll go look at it." She had some sympathy for Lily, but she was secretly figuring what the balance was on her Master Charge and how she could get a cash advance.

Lily was very creative. All that day, which fortunately there wasn't much left of, Lily managed to keep them busy.

They went for a walk on the strip, which is about all there is to Las Vegas, they ate dinner and they went to a show, Gabe Kaplan and Marilyn McCoo with Billy Davis, Jr. But in the morning, Danni got up first. She would be careful; she would just look around at everything. As she rounded the corner by the mink shop, she could already feel it, the ozone crackle of the possible jackpot. She held back. She walked around the whole casino. She watched the blackjack games, the craps shooters, the roulette. She tried to figure out Keno, but she didn't have the concentration. Finally she wandered through the slots, the nickel machines with the blue-haired ladies holding buckets of nickels. Better yet, the quarter slots with people of every description holding equally large buckets of quarters. The dollar slots -- her eyes lit up, she was home. She went to change her ten dollars. By the time Lily found her she had already found the bank teller windows and got a cash advance on her charge card. She was already back at the dollar slots, watching the dollars pour out and the jackpot light go on for some lucky soul. The addiction had taken hold. None of Lily's suggestions worked now. Danni clung stubbornly to the mechanical arm of her new friend. As Lily watched, fifty dollars came tumbling out of the machine. Now Lily started to get caught up in the excitement. She went to get her money changed and the sisters stood side-by-side pulling and hoping, pulling and hoping, occasionally glancing sideways to see what was happening with the other sister's machine. Danni had fed thirty dollars back into the machine in no time. She had had a few small wins and those had also disappeared into the voracious metal maw. Reluctantly Danni quit while she still had twenty dollars. The silver dollars were so nice and heavy, so solid, so different from paper money. She couldn't stand to lose the whole pile. This time it was Danni who had to tear Lily away. That was the end of their gambling. They stayed clear of the casino after that and went to the pool again. They went to dinner and the Follies Bergère. The next morning they carried their own bags down to the desk, then out to the curb. Danni stayed with the bags while Lily went to get the car. At this point Lily would have given up her dreams of regal splendor for the clean towels, which had never arrived.

It was a rather somber ride home. Lily's vacation was almost over. She would be leaving for home in two days. Danni felt homesick already. They didn't have any plans to visit landmarks on the way home, but when they hit Lake Havasu City and saw that the London Bridge had been reconstructed there, they had to stop. It was eerie to see the Victorian Bridge sitting there in the middle of the desert, but as soon as they stepped out on the bridge Danni was transported back to 17th century England. All around her were coaches and ladies in voluminous, long dresses walking on the arms of gentlemen in tails and top hats and white gloves. The Victorian lamps along the bridge were glowing softly and Danni could swear she saw fog. There are ghosts on that bridge and they don't care if they're in the middle of London or the middle of the desert.

After that they drove straight back to Tucson. This time they knew how long it would take. They took steps to combat the heat, which they knew would be fierce even though they were not returning by the route through the badlands. They had a cooler with sodas in the car. Danni had a terry cloth hat, which she held under the faucet at the gas stations where they stopped. She didn't care how she looked. She couldn't afford to bake her brains. They were her only gift and she protected them the way a pianist protects her hands. Lily was embarrassed. Sisters! We're stuck with them, thank goodness. They arrived home in pretty good shape this time.

Danni took Lily to the swap meet, to Nogales, Mexico, took her to dinner one last time and then it was time to put her on the plane for home with a hug, an awkward kiss and messages for everybody. Summer was over. It was time to register for Fall courses. Time to get back to Perez and time to get prepared for the comprehensive exam Danni had to pass to earn her degree.

15
Tucson

Danielle was really happy for Kate. She had finished her Master's, she had gotten a promotion at Social Services and Kate and Stuart were talking about living together, maybe getting married. Danni spent the whole day in her kitchen whipping up a large pan of lasagna and singing at the top of her lungs accompanied by Roberta Flack. Mary was at the library. Kate loved lasagna, Danni knew she did. She was stopping by later to go grocery shopping with Danni and Danni planned to present her with the aromatic Italian delight as soon as she arrived.

Somewhere in the middle of "Killing Me Softly", Ann, one of Danielle's young neighbors stopped by. It was Saturday, Ann usually was with her boyfriend but he was moving. His employer had transferred him. He wanted her to quit her job and move north with him, but he wasn't talking marriage. Amy, Ann's roommate, thought she would be nuts to go. For some reason Amy didn't like Ann's boyfriend, Steve. Danni thought Amy was perhaps jealous, that she didn't want her life to change right now, and that she would be lonely without Ann. She was on the verge of giving one of her pithy pieces of advice borrowed from Amanda, the Sufi philosopher, when, fortunately, Kate arrived.

"Hi Danni," she called through the screen door, "you ready? Oh, sorry, I didn't realize you had company."

"That's O. K.," Ann said, "I have to go anyway."

"No don't go," Kate said, "we don't have to leave right this minute."

"Kate, this is Ann; Ann, Kate," Danni said.

"Hi Ann."

"Hello Kate...I really do have to go, I have some laundry in the machine," Ann said, "I'll talk to you later, Danni. Think about what I asked you?"

"O. K., Ann, but I don't know if I'll come up with anything, I haven't had great success with relationships," Danni pointed out, "See you later," Danni said as Ann moved off toward the laundry room.

Kate caught Danni's eye and raised her eyebrows, but for once Danni kept her mouth shut. She just inclined her head slightly to one side and palms up, shrugged her shoulders.

"Geez, Danni, you don't look quite ready to go shopping," Kate said when she saw Danni's apron and the state of her kitchen.

"It won't take me long, have some tea...you sound awful...what's wrong?" Danni asked as she rinsed and stacked dishes.

"I get a sinus infection like this every fall," Kate said, "this is a really bad one, I can't smell food or taste it. Last year the doctor had to pack my sinuses, they'll probably have to do it again this year."

"Well Kate, I have a surprise for you," Danni said ruefully, as she pulled the browned bubbling lasagna from the oven. "Happy Master's, congratulations on the job. At least Stuart will enjoy this. You'll have to pick it up on the way back, it's too hot."

"That was really nice of you, Danni," Kate said, " I wish I could smell it. I know Stuart will really appreciate it. Maybe I can freeze it until my sinuses clear up."

Danielle was running back and forth between the kitchen and the bathroom. She removed her apron on the way out of the kitchen; she was in the bathroom next washing her face. Now she was back in the kitchen, at the table, in front of a portable mirror putting on fresh make-up. Kate just kept talking to her like she was standing still, raising and lowering her voice as necessary.

"Are you registered for classes, Danni? When do they start?" Kate said.

"Yep, classes start in two days, bet you're glad they're starting without you," Danni called as she sprinted to the bathroom, "I got an out-of-state tuition waiver. They let me pay the in-state fee, isn't that great?"

"Danni, you don't have to run, I'm not in that big a hurry," Kate told Danni as she rushed back towards the kitchen with her make-up, "How's Perez? Have you been back to work?"

"Yes, I've been back," Danni said, suddenly serious, "that man is headed for disaster. Nothing's changed. He's still hardly ever there. He still stops by and takes all the cash, Gina's still very unhappy and so Perez is always either angry or depressed. I'm more sure than ever that he's into drugs, cocaine I think. Something's going to happen, I know it. I've tried to talk to Perez, but he won't listen to me. I know I should get out of there but somehow I have to see it through to the end. The other day Perez got real serious. We were alone in the office. Perez said that he wanted to leave his share of the store to me in case anything happened to him. It gave me the creeps."

"He said that?" Kate asked. "What did you say?"

"I told him to please not do that, I told him nothing was going to happen to him, which I wish I believed, and I told him I couldn't accept anything I hadn't earned. It gave me the shivers for more reasons than one," Danni said. "I'm ready, Kate, let's go."

"But what did he say when you said no?" Kate asked.

"He just said Danni, no matter what anyone says, you're all right."

"Well, what does that mean?" Kate said.

"I'm not sure about the 'no matter what anyone says' part but the rest I took for high praise. Perez really meant it and I'm not sure why, but it made me feel good that he felt that way."

In the car the conversation somehow got around to Carson. Danni couldn't stop herself. When she got with Kate, even though she knew Kate disapproved, she had to pump her for info. She knew Kate couldn't resist helping, and after all she was Danni's only connection to Carson. Danni wasn't even sure why she still wanted to know about him. She wasn't walking around feeling broken hearted. But he was her cowboy.

"Well, I heard Colleen hasn't been around lately," Kate told her, "apparently Carson's been calling her but she hasn't been answering her phone. He hasn't seen her in a couple of weeks."

Danni should have felt bad for him, but she didn't. Somehow she felt she would see him again. Kate just said she didn't know what Danielle saw in Carson. She didn't think Carson and Danni had a whole lot in common. But that's what Kate always said.

"What about you and Stuart, huh," Danni said, "what's going on with you two."

Kate rarely talked about her relationship with Stuart. She didn't analyze, ask for advice or complain. Now she just smiled and said they were looking at houses to rent.

Danni knew better than to comment, all she asked was, "have you found anything you like yet?"

"Not yet," Kate said. Subject closed.

They finished shopping. When Kate dropped Danni off at the apartment she picked up the luscious lasagna that smelled like sawdust through her poor swollen sinuses, thanked Danni for it, and said she would call soon. She headed off toward her dilapidated hacienda at the beautiful foot of the Rincons.

16
Tucson

Mary had a friend coming from New York. Her name was Rachel. They had been best friends since high school. At the beginning of the visit Rachel seemed likable. She was a perky, petite woman, intelligent, with a gamin face and a wry sense of humor. Mary took Rachel sightseeing so Danni saw little of them, although she did go shopping with them at La Placida Village and they all went one day to the Tucson Art Museum and out to lunch. However, since Rachel arrived their teenage friend, Tim, the one with the hormones, was always underfoot. Danni was jealous; she couldn't believe it but she was. Whenever she was around there was Rachel, soaking up all that sexual energy that Mary and Danni had once had all to themselves. Men are so fickle, Danielle thought. By the time Rachel left Danni unintentionally, but definitely, felt cool towards her and pretty silly about it too. Sometimes the dynamics between women are as weird or weirder than the dynamics between men and women. Of course, she forgot how greasy she and Mary had looked during most of Tim's visits. But it did seem that everything was adding up for a big case of the blues. And Danielle was feeling restless too. Maybe it just had to do with the way time was suddenly flying by. It was September, almost October. Just November and December left and then Danni had to go home. She had thought about staying but after all, she had signed that legal piece of paper. And there really was no one to keep her here. Perez was acting more unpredictable by the day. There was nobody home there anymore. Where was the old Perez? Was he hiding, or gone forever?

Danni couldn't stop thinking back to the other day when Perez had come into Sonora Safari with a Mexican bag over his shoulder, one of those woven ones with the fringe hanging off the bottom. He set it on the counter in the store and then he went off into his act. Pretending to be the old Perez, he had flashed his smile a little, danced around a few people and then disappeared, maybe into the bathroom. Danni could tell it was an act, she knew his heart wasn't in it. She didn't think he should leave his Mexican bag sitting there on the store counter so she had picked it up to carry it into the office. It was heavy. She had almost dropped it. It had an odd weighty shape inside it. Danielle knew that shape, not by touch, she knew it by sight. But her vision synapses traded messages with her tactile synapses and her blood went cold. She knew what it was. She had carried it carefully into the office. Fred was there.

"Fred," she had said, calmly and quietly, "Perez has a gun. There's a gun in here."

"You've been watching too much TV," Fred had said, and left to take the jeep for gas. Tour season was starting up again.

But Danielle was sure it was a gun and she was very scared. She didn't know what to do. She didn't know what Perez planned. Maybe she should tell Riley. Did Perez plan to use it on Gina or himself, or Gina and then himself or was there someone else? She had put the bag down on the table by the window and tried to do some work. After all everyone around here couldn't fall apart. But she wasn't doing very well at faking it. Perez didn't notice. When he wandered back from the bathroom, or wherever, he seemed distracted.

"Danni, where's my bag?" Perez had asked.

Danni had pointed to the table. Perez hadn't even noticed that it wasn't where he left it. He had picked it up off the table with no special care and hung it back on his shoulder.

"Gotta run, Danni, will you lock up?" he had called, without waiting for an answer, and then he was gone.

Danni had tried to shake it off. Maybe she had been watching too much television. He hadn't acted like he was especially angry or depressed, just like he was busy, thinking of other things. She wouldn't talk to Riley yet. She decided she'd wait awhile. But it was unsettling, depressing. After all, roller coasters don't only go up.

And there was the man situation. That wasn't doing well either. She certainly couldn't claim that love was keeping her here, not even lust. She hadn't had a date in weeks. Even the aging James with his paunch was starting to look good. After all, he did have a beautiful '57 Chevy.

School was going well. Danni usually could succeed in school even when other parts of her life were in a shambles. She had met two new women in her classes who she really liked. They were taking the same exam that Danni was taking. Although they were from different backgrounds, there was an instant rapport between them. But doing well in school wasn't enough, after all school would end in December. She fully expected to earn her degree and she couldn't stay for a doctorate right now. She couldn't afford it. In fact, Danni was not sure she could afford to go home either. She had spent it all; even the Master Card cupboard was bare. What she got as half her salary from her job at home and what she earned at Sonora Safari just covered her expenses. Maybe Mom and Dad would help. Danni knew she would go home. It already felt like things were coming to an end here, overblown, gone to seed, gone sour. But there were the Poconos to consider. Danni knew she could not drive through the Poconos in early January. Well, she wasn't going to start thinking about black ice or going home yet. She still had three months. Leaving was a long way off.

When nothing came of the incident with Perez and the gun Danielle started to feel sure that she had been wrong. There was some other explanation for what her senses had reported. She remembered this exhibit at a nature museum she had been to where you put your hands in through these holes and felt ordinary natural objects. Then, after you guessed, you could open up the top to see if you guessed right. It was surprising how your sense of touch alone could lead you astray. Danni put this on the plus side of the ledger, maybe she didn't have all the facts, maybe her intuition was faulty.

Also on the plus side was Ann's invitation for Danni to go on a motorcycle ride with her and Steve and a friend of theirs to Tombstone. Danni had never been on a motorcycle. If she had ever been on one she would have realized that it is not quite the thing for someone who rides in an enclosed car with her fingers spread over her eyes, but of course, ignorance is bliss, and there was a man involved. Danni was not normally an abnormally man-crazy female, but she was feeling unwanted and she needed a little masculine attention. So the plans moved ahead and Danni's spirits started to rise. Danni put away the blues; she tabled her intuition of impending doom. She blanked out the black ice season that followed gorgeous autumn in the Poconos and she tucked Perez's possible insanity away in a corner of her mind. She dove into her last semester in Tucson.

On the day of the motorcycle trip Ann and Steve's friend, Mark, showed up. He was a veteran biker with a weathered face and a weathered bike. Danni knew nothing about bikes, but she could tell it was a big one. Mark was a skinny malink with blond hair and a small bald spot at the top of his head. He was awkward and not very talkative. Danni knew she could eliminate falling in love and just enjoy the day. By the time they dressed her in someone else's winter jacket, which made her look like a pudgy blonde Eskimo, stuck some boots on her feet and added a wool skull cap, Danni knew love was out of the question for Mark too. She looked ridiculous. She didn't want to go looking like that. But then they told her she wouldn't have to wear all that stuff until they were on their way back. It would be much colder by then, and darker. Danni had no experience to fall back on or she would have realized the key word was colder. She didn't pick up on the cues.

She wasn't scared on the way to Tombstone. Looking out over the desert was too beautiful. It didn't look strange at all anymore, or dull, or dusty. She remembered very well how the desert had looked to her those first few weeks in Tucson, but now she loved it. It had so many colors, not just green and gray and brown, but purple, blue, pink, orange and yellow. It had a mellow palette, the colors always soft and diffuse. The subtlety actually made the strong greens and blues and browns of home seem over-rich and greedy, wasteful nature spilling her seeds with no particular parsimony or care. Here there was an economy of nature, a scarcity that made all life have extra value because it was lived at greater risk.

Here in the desert nature was not frugal when it came to the sky. It was huge, airy and clear, filling nine-tenths of the huge heavenly semi dome in every direction, 180º of sky dwarfing the earth, even the distant mountains, until you felt like you were in one of those sealed paperweights with the water, on God's desk, only this paperweight had no snow flakes, only a couple of little floaty clouds way up high.

Riding through it on a motorcycle you were actually in it. It was all around you. Danni felt a bit self-conscious about hugging a strange man and looking like a motorcycle mama, but the day was so sunny, the surroundings so gorgeous and the situation so new that she put her self-consciousness aside and just rode with the rpm's.

They stopped at a diner at a crossroads in the middle of the desert for lunch and then they were back on the road, with just the desert around them, her favorite ocatilla and the organ pipe cactus, the saguaros and the sky above them, and a warm male body to hold on to. She liked it.

When they got to Tombstone they had to pull over while the guys locked up their guns in their saddlebags. Danni hadn't noticed the guns. The guys had shoulder holsters on under their jackets. Danni had decided she did not like guns. By now she was definitely gun shy. It was very obvious that guns were still accepted casually in the 'West' but for a girl from the Northeast they meant tragedy, violence and destruction. Danni's experiences linked guns with crime and death. Seeing the guns brought back her fears about Perez. She was glad when the guns were locked in the saddlebags. She was glad that in Tombstone you still couldn't bring your guns to town.

It would have been fun to walk the wooden sidewalks in long dresses with hair upswept and a tiny hat with blue roses and a veil riding high on her forehead. But this was 1970. The women were dressed like the men in jeans and flannel shirts. They wore boots and they had tousled hair.

"Well what'd'ya think, Danni?" Ann asked.

Danni wasn't sure whether Ann meant Mark or the motorcycle ride but she decided to take the safe course. "It was great, it makes you feel so free"

"Isn't this neat," Ann said, "you really feel like you're in the old West don't'cha?"

"Oh, look," Danni said, "there's the General Store. Where are we going? Why don't we go in there?"

"We're going to the saloon," Ann said, "it's right over there. Maybe we can see the General Store later."

Danielle would have insisted on seeing the General Store, told the guys they would meet them at the saloon later, but since she hadn't seen any of Tombstone and since she was hot and thirsty she decided the saloon was a good idea. The saloon had swinging wooden doors. You couldn't help but think of "Gunsmoke." Danni expected to see Miss Kitty when they pushed open the doors. It wasn't quite authentic. She saw beer taps behind the bar and there was an electric Coors sign, but other than that it could have been 1850. There was the player piano and there was the staircase going up in the back corner. There were wooden bar stools at the bar, round wooden tables with spindle-armed chairs filled the room and there was sawdust on the floor. It was dark after the brilliance of the day.

"You ladies can't come in here," the guys kidded, probably wishing it was still male territory.

"Try and stop us," Ann said. "I'll get the sheriff."

They sat in the comfortable wooden gloom for a while sipping their beers, the guys talking intently to each other. Ann resumed the conversation she had started week ago as if no time had intervened. Danni knew she'd have to say something this time.

"What should I do, Danni. Now you've spent a little more time with him. Should I give up my job and go with him? Now they've offered me a promotion. I'm more confused than ever. Amy is still really against it."

"Why is she so against it?" Danni asked.

I guess she feels that no woman should ever become totally dependent on a man. She should keep her own residence until she's married and she should always have a job so she has her own money. Besides, she thinks Steve is very domineering."

"Is he?" Danni asked. She thought Amy made sense but was maybe a little too paranoid.

"He listens to me," Ann said. "Sometimes he does things with me that I want to do. He's not always happy when I go out with Amy, but he does let me go."

He was so handsome and he seemed so nice that Danni didn't know what to say. She really didn't know enough to give advice. But Ann was waiting. So Danni fell back, as she had intended to before, on the wise conundrums of Amanda's Sufis.

"Ann, listen to yourself, you already know what you want to do. You've already made your decision."

Danni might as well have packed Ann's bags. She might as well have bought her a housewarming gift. She knew very well what Ann would do with her advice. It didn't help to know that she probably would have done the same without Danni's advice. Danni wished already that she had kept her mouth shut.

143

The guys were obviously ready to make a move.

"Mark's got a friend up the road a piece," Steve said. (That's how they talk out West.) "We're gonna stop by and see if he's in."

Well it seemed that, although their wishes were not being consulted, at least the two women were not being completely ignored. They trooped out to the bikes and sped off 'down the road a piece.' When they got there they parked the bikes across the street and Mark went in alone. He came right back out.

"He's not home, let's just head back," Mark said when he came back.

"O. K., saddle up," Steve said, (more technical cowboy-motorbike lingo.)

Danni never did find out what they would have done if Mark's friend was home, but she figured it would have been a drug buy. By now she had decided that most unexplained behavior was drug related. She was relieved that Mark's friend had not been home. She and Mark were still virtually strangers, in spite of the fact that she had been clinging to his body all day. That had been a survival matter, not an intimacy matter.

> *Get your motor running,*
> *Head out on the highway,*
> *Looking for adventure*
> *Or whatever comes your way...* Steppenwolf

The bikes vibrated and ran with a throaty roar. It was like straddling something that was alive. They were going back the fast route, on the highway. They told Danni to put the winter jacket on, the gloves, the hat. Danni knew what she looked like. Her vanity did not want to have anything to do with the getup, but she put it on anyway. She'd have to trust their experience in these matters.

Thank goodness she did. The trip home was a nightmare. The night air that rushed past them was freezing; it stung and bit at any piece of uncovered flesh. What was uncovered was Danni's face. She hid it behind Mark's body, but he was so thin it didn't help. All day Mark made fun of Steve saying he didn't have a real motorcycle, he was a sissy, he couldn't take it. Steve had a large wrap-around windshield on his bike. He had a radio behind that windshield. Ann and Steve rode in a wind-free environment with musical accompaniment. Danielle would have given anything to be on a sissy bike at the moment. Her face became more and more frozen. She felt it harden in an unattractive mask of pain and shock. For a while it tingled excruciatingly every time the wind hit it, but then it just became numb and ugly. She held on, waiting for it to be over. It seemed to take forever. She wasn't even scared; she was too busy trying to save her face. She thought it was going to fall off. She remembered when she was a child and she used to make faces by pulling down her nose and stretching out her lips with her baby fingers, her mother used to say 'what if your face froze that way?' That's what she thought about all the way home. Would her face ever thaw and look normal. Now Danni understood why Mark's face looked like corrugated cardboard. Was the beating worth it? Obviously her answer would be different from Mark's. Danielle didn't care if she ever saw another motorcycle.

Finally they were back at the apartments on N. Swan. Danni climbed stiffly off the bike. She was so frozen she didn't even care that she looked plump, rumpled, hairless and hard. She did remember her manners and invite everyone in. By the time she had removed the offending jacket and replaced it with her apron, by the time she had added the remains of the pot roast to the spaghetti sauce and held her aching face over the steam escaping from the spaghetti pot she started to feel warmer.

They all sat on the living room floor around the coffee table and ate like they were starving with their plates held close to their mouths just shoveling it in (except Danni who still couldn't eat that fast). They had cold beers and the TV was on. Danni started to feel human. She thought about combing her hair and washing her face but she decided she would rather get rid of these guys and just go to bed. They really had nothing to say to each other. For once Danni felt old, she felt like their mother, although Mark was probably her age. Luckily they didn't stay. After they ate they pleaded exhaustion and made their getaway. Danni was an accomplice.

Somehow in the morning the experience again became an adventure and Danni grew more impressed with her bravery as Mary's reactions grew more admiring. Danielle thanked her lucky stars that Mark didn't invite her to go again, though. It's true you may forget the pain, but you don't deliberately touch the stove a second time.

Ann did quit her job soon after that and move north with Steve. Amy was very angry with Danni. Amy implied that Danni talked Ann into it. Danni knew she certainly didn't talk her out of it. Amy also seemed to be suggesting that Steve was not the perfect partner, that he was extremely jealous and possessive and therefore physically and emotionally abusive. Danni wasn't sure if that was what Amy was saying, but she vowed again, for the umpteenth time to never give anyone advice again, however cryptic. She also began to believe that, truly, as the song says, "a good man is hard to find."

Mary was at loose ends since Rachel left. At the beginning of a new semester you always felt that you had so much time. Then just when you started filling that time with interesting and normal things to do the avalanche began, the snow job, paper snow. And then you just had to stop doing all those things that you started doing in that spare time and head back to the library. Danielle wasn't used to Mary being at home but now there were the two of them, rattling around, cooking breakfast, trying to use the bathroom, heading for the telephone and wanting to tune in different TV shows at the same times. At first they were in each other's way. But after a few days it got kind of companionable. Danni started to enjoy having Mary's company at breakfast; they went out to the pool together and lazed in the sun. The fall sun was kinder than the summer sun. They chatted back and forth from the depths of their lounge chairs. Danni got Mary to talk a bit about her days in the sisterhood. Mary had liked the work, which was a lot like social work, what she had decided she didn't like was chastity. She wanted a husband and children. She was very bright and that had something to do with why she chose to go to graduate school, but it was also her halfway house. It was a sort of sheltered steppingstone back to the world at large. Mary's habit of caring about people and wanting to be useful would never change.

By the time the paper blizzard descended Mary was brown and no longer had circles under her eyes, Danni was at least golden and they were more comfortable with each other than they had been, which was how they ended up going to the Halloween party together.

What a party! They didn't have them quite this wild in Syracuse. It was too cold at the end of October. Someone at school told Danni and Mary they just had to go. The house was not huge but it was filled with people, most in costume, some not. What impressed Danni most was the second kitchen in the backyard. It was built with only one wall and a roof with porch-like supports in front. It had running water and a stove, refrigerator, the works. Someone explained to Danni that it was a Mexican custom to have an outdoor and indoor kitchen, although the modern appliances were an American adaptation.

They had a D.J. at the party and there were prizes for the best costumes. Danni and Mary went sort of as sightseers. They didn't wear costumes and they didn't really know anyone. Most of these people were not college people. They were young native Tucsonians, a very hard breed to find. Mary and Danni also went looking for romance, but it's hard to fall in love with an ape-man or a ghost. Since Tucson is still fairly hot at Halloween a lot of people went in for a semi-clothed look. Danni was sitting on the couch watching the judging. Mary was seated on the arm of a chair, which sat at right angles to the couch. She was right next to the judging. They had seen a couple dressed like a light socket and a plug. It was very creatively done with stuffed fabrics, a sort of quilted look. The woman could plug into his socket while they danced and when she plugged in, her necklace, made of tiny Christmas tree lights lit up. Danni was sure they would get first prize. Then Danni noticed Mary waving her arms and pointing her finger behind her open palm. Right in front of Mary's eyes (eye level) was the bare butt of a guy dressed only in a cocktail apron. There went first prize.

And there went Danni and Mary. They left by the front door giggling. The man hunt was over. This was a little too much man for either of them. That was the last time Danni and Mary peeped their heads out together from underneath the now imminent paper blizzard for quite a while.

17
Tucson

Megan and Skye were Danielle's new classmates. They were, all three, in the last semester of the same Early Childhood program, which meant they were in several required classes together. They were scheduled to take their exams at the same time. They were in the same frantic state of exam delirium; their confidence waxed and waned together like the subtle desert seasons.

Danielle was immensely impressed with and infatuated by these two. Megan, a tiny soft-spoken woman with hidden steel and indefatigable energy, Danni saw as incredibly mature and capable. She ran a large and lovely home for her husband and three young boys. She had married a Mexican professional, a Doctor, and they lived an affluent Tucson lifestyle of which Danni had had only glimpses. Once Danni had visited a professor's home with another student who was housesitting. It had been a huge modern adobe with a black glass dining table that seated twelve. All the chairs matched and there wasn't a captain's chair in the crowd. Her apartment would have fit in the kitchen. It had had a slatted wooden deck on several levels with sunken swimming pool on the top layer. Danni had also seen one of the older mansions, lined with Mexican tiles, when she went to an estate sale. Megan's house was different, it was a house to live in, but it was equally impressive. Megan and Jose´ had a gallery of sculptures, Mexican folk art, and beautiful prints. Their floors were tiled with authentic terra cotta tiles; they had a huge fireplace, although Danni could not imagine when they would use it. It was a vivid house, a lively house and a comfortable house and Danni was amazed that Megan had created it, that she organized and ran it with such warmth and grace. Megan didn't seem old enough or formal enough. To

Danni, she seemed to embody the same free spirit as Danni's single friends. Yet she was the calm, strong center of her own loving family and she was as natural with her three young, handsome boys as a desert breeze against the fine willows. Megan seemed surprised that Danni admired her. She thought her lifestyle was confining and hopelessly conventional. She felt she was the butterfly in the cocoon waiting to be released. Danni felt that Megan was born a rare butterfly, but apparently didn't know it.

Skye was everything her name suggested, everything Danni tried to be, longed to be. She was tall and blonde and lithe and she was a truly independent person. Apparently no one had ever told her anything was impossible and therefore nothing was. Of the bold adventurous spirit, the truly liberated female they all wanted to be, she was the genuine article. She had a masculine directness and dash, but she was as feminine as a crewel tapestry. She came from the Midwest, where she had obviously been enormously and lavishly spoiled, but the only thing hayseed about her was the glorious sun drenched wheat field she tucked casually back over her shoulder or behind her ear from whence it always slid forward to hang as a shining curtain beside her golden profile. "I will not be envious," Danni told herself, but not too successfully. Skye wore weathered blue jeans with the knees ripped out as if those long, lean limbs could not be bound. She wore denim work shirts; with lacy undershirts peeping out and leather work boots or leather sandals, the changing footwear the only concession to the varied settings she occupied. A friend had given her a house to live in rent-free if she would work to fix it up. When she wasn't studying, she was laying floors or hanging wallboard. She talked Danni into helping her once and they spent a whole day with rollers on long handles putting pink paint over the yellowed stucco exterior of Sky's borrowed house. Danni's arms ached but Skye seemed tireless. She talked and joked as she splashed pink polka dots over the green leaves of the bushes, which she did not bother to prune away from the house. Danni wondered what Skye's friend would say, but Skye never seemed to give it a thought, she just smiled her sly-boots smile, and cracked another joke and another beer. Danielle knew Skye was young, that she had not yet failed, that she had never yet been afraid to be alone with knives, but she also recognized that Skye had been nurtured to a brand of brash confidence that Danni might never attain.

For Danielle it was another unlikely trio; no wonder she believed in the supernatural. Admittedly, it was uncanny to watch the pattern unfold, unpremeditated, time after time. Megan adopted Danni and Skye into the family, enveloping them with inexhaustible intimacy. She made huge breakfasts and invited them to eat en *familia* at the enormous carved dining room table, another Mexican folk art piece altered from some dark tropical wood by a careful and creative artisan. They ate for hours and drank coffee and talked, the adults and the children together. Then they would clear the table, take care of the leftovers, stack the dishes in the dishwasher and switch it on. The children would disappear, the textbooks and note cards would take the place of the food and each of the three would spend a portion of the afternoon drilling the other two in their topic for the day. It was perhaps sinful to turn the pursuit of dim ascetic scholars into such a dual feast but it satisfied.

In Danni's new lifestyle Sonora Safari once again seemed out of place but she still went there faithfully. Megan and Skye both agreed with Kate that she should quit but Danni was paralyzed like her little green lizard friend, who sprawled helplessly on the wall each day after he ran out from under the blue Toyota shade umbrella. Besides she felt she ran the entire operation now, without her the partners would see the trouble Perez was in. She knew that might be the best thing but she felt protective, she felt Perez was in danger somehow. So she watched with horrified fascination and waited for the end that she knew was imminent.

The partner's wives came in now, occasionally, and helped out at the counter but they also seemed either unaware of the real problem, or as frozen as Danni. Danni didn't know what Perez told them, what tune he danced to that convinced them to accept his absences. No one talked about it. There were still very few cash receipts to bank although all the checks were there. However, only Danni kept the books, did the banking and saw the accountant. The partners still left it to Perez to handle the financial end, why Danni could not imagine. They probably didn't even know about the missing cash. Danni suspected that there was one partner, however, who was the recipient of all that cash and it wasn't Perez.

She saw Perez only once during those several endless weeks and he looked deflated. His energetic wiriness appeared gaunt now without the animated jazz ballet of his adrenaline-induced gyrations. His cheekbones were sunken with dark canyons underneath. His hair was flat and dull, no longer the crackling apex of his inner fire. He was all waif now and Danni longed to adopt him. He needed emotional CPR, he needed brutal honesty, he needed a rubber room.

"Perez, are you OK," Danni couldn't help but say.

"Gotta fin' somephen' I lef in the back room," Perez mumbled, not looking at her, shuffling on past.

"Everybody's been trying to find you," Danni nagged, "the tour groups are backing out."

"Leave me alone, Dan, I'm inna hurry," he practically whined.

Danni couldn't stand it. She hadn't felt this way since Lawrence of Arabia when Peter O'Toole underwent his transformation from demagogue to paranoid catatonic. She couldn't stand to see him this way. She had known Perez was not stable from the beginning. She hadn't been really comfortable with his original routine either, but to see him like this, it broke her heart. She didn't know what to do. She knew he wasn't her project. She knew he was over her head.

She also didn't think any of the people he had charmed would stick around for this Perez. Did he have no true friends or was he just beyond where friendship reached? He went out through the shop without saying good-bye.

Danni talked on the phone endlessly. The customers wanted to know what was wrong with Perez. "He's just busy," Danni would say. "He's going through some hard times," she would explain. Even Jake hadn't seen him, although apparently Gina, even though she had kicked him out, still saw him occasionally.

So Danielle spent the early part of the fall semester, moving alternately in sunshine and in shade, harsh chiaroscuro of desert landscapes. She was experiencing simultaneously both the best and the worst life had to offer, the pinnacle and the pits. But on the pinnacle she was a participant; of the pits, only an observer. She was beginning to realize if something was happening to someone you knew, or even maybe loved, it wasn't necessarily happening to you. She felt guilty that she felt relieved about that, but she couldn't help it.

18
Tucson

When the phone rang in the middle of the night, as soon as Danielle was awake enough to answer it, she knew from her sinking heart what it would be about. It was Perez. Riley found him in a motel room. He had put a bullet through his own head. [The roller coaster neared the bottom of a vertical drop.]

Because of all Danni's premonitions, she wasn't surprised, but she was shocked. Standing there staring at the phone after she put it back on its cradle, she had the sensation that she was losing her new, hard-won grip on reality. Her body felt insubstantial, she was afraid there in the dark. Her throat closed, her old terrors returned. She couldn't swallow. She made herself walk to the light, which she knew was on the end table in the living room. She switched it on. She sat in the sling- back canvas chair, head bent forward over her knees. She massaged her throat. She refused to fall back into her pre-Tucson state when it felt as if there was nothing to live for, when she had felt exhausted by living and feeling, when she felt she had already lived enough and learned enough. She willed away the hammock with the red-dripping wrists, the pools of blood on the sand, grass, and concrete underneath. She gripped each wrist tightly with the opposite hand and squeezed. She rose and made herself some tea and watched the sun rise beyond the jasmine as she sipped. The tea did go down, reluctantly, harshly, but inevitably. Her throat muscles gradually relaxed. She still felt slightly unreal. When the sun was up, she decided she would skip classes and lay by the pool. She needed the heat.

At first she was sorry about her decision. She didn't want anyone to see her, to talk to her. She wanted to be there, but invisibly. Something in her longed to remain unreal. But

Tina, the bald baby of the young couple next door was there in her playpen under the porch roof on the front of the bathhouse. Her little golden face glowed with pleasure and health. She was playing by herself while her mother swam but she was happy; babbling and gumming her toys; piling things up and waving them down; powerful, a builder and a destroyer. Danni's tension relaxed under the assault of the melting sun and the baby's cheerfulness. Her skin could not tingle in all this heat; it was impossible to feel cold. When Tina's mother, Bev, got out of the pool and said hi to Danni she heard herself answer in a normal tone of voice.

Eventually as Danni sat under the bathhouse porch with Tina and Bev, James, of all people, the Lawrence Welk with a paunch, joined them. Bev offered Danni a beer. They sat back in their lounge chairs and sipped their beers comfortably, talking sporadically and lazily of the everyday; raising kids, how hard it is to hang on to money; commenting on especially precocious activities of baby Tina. By supper time Danni felt whole again, although angry that she had, in her temporarily relaxed and boozy state agreed to go up "A" mountain with James in the '57 Chevy on Saturday. Everyone had to go there, he said. The college students made that "A" and painted it white. You could see the whole city from there. There were hang gliders. Danni had been so grateful for her returning sanity she had been carried away. Oh well, he didn't seem so bad after spending a whole day around him.

Now Danielle was worried that, although she had never used even a dime of the Sonora Safari assets, she would come under suspicion when the partners discovered how much money was missing. She felt bad about Perez. He had needed help no one, including her, could or would give. But at least she wasn't suspended any more. She didn't have to wait and watch the destruction. It was complete. And Perez was, perhaps, at peace.

The partners held a meeting. They wanted Danni to teach them how to do the books. Danni finally had to explain their financial situation to them. She told them about Perez and the cash receipts. She told them about the big shipments. She showed them how much money the checks had brought in. Fortunately, they seemed to take the news calmly. They seemed to accept that Perez was the problem and that Danni had not been in on the action. But Danni felt terrible, she felt awful about Perez, she felt guilty that she had let the situation go so far, and she was angry that she had stayed when she had known she should leave. Still she held back. She didn't mention, even then, even to Riley that she thought Perez had been using the cash receipts to buy dope from one of the partners. She had no proof and, of course, she was scared. Besides, what if Riley was the one?

Whenever Danielle thought back to her year in Tucson, it was like looking at a movie on a split screen. There was the relatively normal world of the university and her friends and her studies; and then there was the relative insanity of Sonora Safari. She was two Danni's, the one who made healthy choices, and this other Danni who was attracted to dangerous people and events, this coming-back-to-life, roller coaster Danni. She realized that it was tiring, if not down-right life threatening to not accept that bad people are bad; to not accept that some people are self-destructive or just selfish, and that it could be demoralizing to be around them. What was there in her, right now, that made people who lived on the edge attractive? Was it because they walked a thin line between life and death?

Danni shakes herself now and she shook herself then, whenever she begins to think like this. That way lay the sharpened knives, the bone in the chicken sandwich, the shallow grave in the woods. So Danni went through the closing motions at Sonora Safari and Death Tours, but she poured her heart into her life on North Swan Road and the University of Arizona.

Megan and Skye were planning to go with Danni to a conference in San Antonio. Dr. Alexander was delivering a paper there, if they attended he had said he would cancel their final paper. Danni thought that if she had to type another paper she would attach mirrors to her clothes and try self-immolation (a new and startling idea only possible in a bright, hot climate). She decided that they were definitely going to the conference. She was broke, however, so she would have to borrow the money to go from her friends. On the last Sunday before the conference they planned to make their final arrangements.

However, before Danni could deal with this humiliation, she had another to face. She still had to go with her middle-aged suitor, owner of the '57 Chevy, to the top of "A" mountain. Nobody could save her, except herself. How did she get herself into these things?

Danielle dressed like a lady for the dreaded tete-a-tete. She wore a flowered skirt, her best little summer-white top and sandals. She also adopted her most aloof, closed demeanor. James was right on time, dressed as casually as middle-aged Lawrence Welk accordion players ever dressed, in sports trousers and a short sleeved button-down shirt. Thank God, he didn't bring flowers or candy.

"Hello Danielle," he said, when she answered the door.

He looked like he was expecting to be asked inside for a few minutes but Danielle had anticipated this eventuality. She started out the door and James had to step aside.

"I'm ready," she said, "let's go." She was very defensive and uptight.

"Well, what did you do today, Danielle," James said.

"Not much," Danielle answered, determined not to thaw.

"You'll really love the view from up here," said poor James, who may not yet have known that he was trying to cut through the deep ice. "Don't people call you anything besides Danielle," he said. "Don't you have another name," he stammered,

Danielle felt bad for him but she didn't dare lower her guard. He did not attract her, if there is an opposite state (as with electrical charges) Danielle felt it. He made her angry; everything he said made her feel meaner. Perhaps certain people have incompatible molecules, their chemistry is alien, their nerve pathways wired backwards. He was repulsive to her, although he was probably a perfectly nice person. She couldn't give him any of herself; an ounce of warmth was squeezed out grudgingly, doled out like rations.

"Nope, that's the only name, I have," she said, then she felt badly, so she offered a crumb, "I suppose people call you Jim." She doled out one little tight smile.

"Yes," he said, "What's wrong, you're so uptight

Oh no, he noticed, Danielle thought.

"Relax," he said, "loosen up, it's Saturday."

That didn't help Danni at all, Saturday was like every other day in the world of the college student. And loosening up wasn't any part of her plan. They plowed on in the '57 Chevy, but it was tough going. That Chevy had never had to beat back such waves of resistance as were rising against it now. The hood seemed to buck. It was literally and figuratively an uphill climb. Finally they were there.

"Look, there's a hang glider," James said in relief. The poor guy was sweating.

Danielle doled out another crumb. "How do they know they won't land on the houses," she asked. "It looks pretty populated down there."

James took her arm, (shudder, shudder) and led her near the edge. They peeped over. Danni could see the flat clear land down below. She couldn't help it, when the first hang glider left the summit and floated in its exciting clean arc over the space beside the mountain, a genuine smile appeared on Danni's face. Danni looked around quickly to see if James had noticed. He had. She put it away as swiftly as she could but he was a starving man. He was a dog in the forest. He was hot on her trail. And heat was exactly what Danni had been trying to avoid. Like a small spark that falls on the woodsman's damp timber, James tried to nurture a flame. He had her pose in front of the Chevy. He took her picture with a Polaroid camera. Danni posed for Mount Rushmore. He had her come over and view the "A", upside-down from this vantagepoint. He told her the story of the college kids again. Danni carefully withheld the crumbs. Finally he got tired of trying.

"Well, I guess we'd better head for home."

Now Danni felt really bad. He never got angry. He stayed gentle and polite. But he took her home without any further attempts to draw her out. Danni was very relieved and very guilty. Probably Danni was the queen of guilt. And why wasn't she ever attracted to nice men?

When she got to her door the phone was ringing. She fumbled with the keys. She was sure that whoever was on it would hang up. But she got there in time. It was Carson. Her heart fell into her shoes -- up-elevator style. Shit. He acted as if they had seen each other only yesterday.

"I'm going hunting tomorrow, wanna go?" He didn't sound like he cared if she went or not.

Danni didn't want to watch someone kill poor, defenseless animals, but she couldn't help herself. She wanted to see Carson.

"Sure, OK, I'll go," she said.

"I'll pick you up about 7:00 tomorrow morning," he said.

God help her, her insides quivered.

"OK, see you then," she said.

"Wear jeans," he said. "Bye, Danni," he said.

She placed the receiver back on the hook and sat down. She was exhausted. Her thermostat was busted and her radiator was leaking. Someone, please explain, she thought. Who's responsible for this, she thought. She knew the answer.

She got a cup of iced tea and pulled out her books. Then she remembered Megan and Skye. They didn't suspect anything when she called and canceled. They made alternate plans for Wednesday evening.

19

Tucson

Danielle thought she would feel awkward when she saw Carson but she didn't. They just picked up where they left off. No discussion. She just resumed her spot on the passenger side of the red Ford truck and smiled at Carson. He leaned over and gave her a little kiss. Bandit peeked over their shoulders through the guns in the gun rack, which hung across the rear window. They were a temporary family.

Danni had no sense of where they went, it was just somewhere in the desert. The earth was dry and yellow but it wasn't as hot as the summer had been. Carson wanted to show her the ruins of an old house he had discovered in the desert. They descended from the truck and wandered around the foundation of the old building. Carson didn't know the history of the place, he just liked it. He knew the desert very well. He was a solitary desert wanderer, who would have been happier in earlier times. He was a frontiersman in his heart, a hunter, a tracker. He was a man who liked a woman, but didn't need her. Women had only one real place in his life and for that he could have been happy just climbing the stairs at the local establishment for a quick romp.

What am I doing here? This is no place for a liberated career woman. She had been raised in the 50's and early 60's, partially transformed by the 70's. She was only partially "liberated". She was always torn between her childhood training as the perfect wife and mother and her temporary vision of a revolutionary future for male-female relationships. Excuses aside, through whatever fatal flaw, right now she wanted to be with this thoroughly unliberated man.

Carson took her picture in front of the ruins. He took her picture in front of the ruins with Bandit. Danni took Carson's picture in front of his truck. They tried to get

Bandit to take a picture of them together but he just sat in front of them with his head cocked to one side. Danni kept the pictures.

They piled back into the truck and drove "down the road a piece" to the killing grounds. Danni could see nothing that offered a clue as to why Carson had picked this spot and she didn't ask as she was determined to be an invaluable mountain woman, following in silence behind her man. This spot was on a low hill covered with short, scrubby bushes and nettles. They were hunting quail but Carson showed her the jackrabbit tracks and she picked out the sika deer prints. He was quietly explaining about some health problem the poor little jackrabbits had been experiencing. Although this saved them from the hunter's guns, it killed them anyway, in much more horrible ways. Bandit, who had been sniffing joyfully in a wide zigzag lope, stopped and grew still and tense. Carson held his rifle horizontally across his body with both hands. Danni stood still. Carson gave a signal and Bandit dashed forward. Birds flew up in panic, twirring softly in their throats. Danni heard the shots. Two birds fell. She helped Carson look for them. She turned her head while he broke their necks and cleaned them right there in the field. He wrapped each separately in newspaper and saved a wing on top of each one. The game wardens required that, he explained. They walked the hills a while longer but they didn't get any more quail. Danni switched off her brain and went with her senses. She was a Navajo woman with her native man, walking whisper-soft behind him in her beaded moccasins. He was young and tanned and muscular and brave. She was soft and pliant and gentle. They would walk together back to the camp. No one else was there. They were on their marriage trip. They would bake the quail over the coals when they got back. They would eat the tender quail meat under the pale moonlight. He would hold her close under the ancient stars and they would giggle together in the cool desert night.

Carson called her back.

"Common, Danni, let's head out."

At the truck he popped the top on a Coors for her, and one for him. They sat with the quail on the seat between them. One hundred yards down the road the game wardens had a roadblock set up. Carson dealt with them. Danni, sunburned and content, rested against the cushions of the front seat in total mindless relaxation.

They had one of her favorite meals, steak marinated in beer, grilled over mesquite wood. Danielle made a salad. They didn't have enough quail to make a meal. Carson would get more and then they'd have that, he told her. They ate in the kitchen and didn't even do the dishes. He led her off directly afterward to the big pine bed. It could have been a fragrant bed of glossy green pine boughs. *Peaceful Easy Feeling.* The Eagles were her lullaby. Ah.

Carson drove her back to North Swan Road early in the morning. It was thundering. In the sky simultaneous lightning bolts flashed from the surrounding mountaintops. They were the white-blue veins in God's magnificent black eyeball. The rain came in torrents, the sky just dropped its load and then it was over. By the time they got to Danni's place the concrete patio was already dry except for a few of the deeper potholes. Carson was holding her hand, fingers entwined. He gave her a light little kiss and he left. Danni stood looking after him with her hand on the doorknob. Damn, damn, damn -- Yippee-kiy-oh-kiy-ay!

Danielle went to class in her neglected little blue dust bucket. The little green lizard dashed from under the Toyota just as he did every time. He eyed her from his alternate spot, clinging to the green concrete wall. "Good-bye, little green lizard," Danni whispered, feeling foolish.

In the parking lot off Speedway she carefully draped the now familiar towel over the steering wheel and rushed across the rich green grass on campus to her class. Megan and Skye were both in this class with her. Danni gave them the hi sign when she walked in. It was too late for talking. This was one of their favorite professors, Dr. Patti Simpson. She loved the book <u>Zen and the Art of Motorcycle Maintenance</u>, she was explaining to them. She liked the juxtaposition of the concreteness of the motorcycle maintenance as an analogy to describe a methodology for the philosophical quest for spiritual truth. It embraced both the simple and the profound of which life is such a rich mixture.

Dr. Simpson was a new mother. She was entranced by her baby girl. She was studying the child's babbling as a case study in natural language acquisition. She made tapes and the whole class listened as the infant grew into each new stage. And so the morning passed in contemplation of the meaning of life and stuff.

Danielle planned to rush out of there because she had to get to Sonora Safari, but as she raised her hand to wave at Megan and Skye, Skye called, "Hold on a minute, Danni." She waited for them.

"I have to get to work."

"Well, let's pick a hotel. We better call and make reservations tonight or we won't have anywhere to stay," Megan said.

Skye wrinkled up her face. She wasn't a planner. She would have slept on a park bench or not slept at all. Danni wanted to stay at the St. Anthony. Megan would call there when she got home.

"Gotta run," Danni said.

When she got to Sonora Safari, Riley's wife Ann was there. She had some questions about the books, then she had to leave. Riley would stop by later, she said, and Fred was around somewhere. She thought that Danni would be done in one or two more days. Ann thought they had the hang of it. A pall of gloom hung over the store. It wasn't the same place. Now it was just a business, like any other business, no drama, no ozone, no loony tunes.

Danielle had decided that Riley was too straight. He could not be the dope dealer who sold the coke to Perez. She was determined to tell him her suspicions today, this very day. She straightened the desk, checked the tour pockets, went out into the store, which was empty. She didn't see Fred anywhere. She wandered back into the office. A bell would ring if anyone came into the shop. She didn't hear Riley when he came into the office. There should have been another bell between the shop and the office. She jumped when he said, "Hi, Danni. What's going on?"

"It's very quiet right now," Danni answered.

"You can leave now if you want," Riley said, "we need you on Thursday and then that can be your last day."

Danielle gathered her courage.

"Sit down a minute, Riley. I want to talk to you."

"OK, Danni." He sat in the chair across from her desk where Jake used to sit.

The only way to tell it is to jump right in, Danni told herself.

"Riley, I think someone here was selling coke to Perez. I think he was giving all that cash to someone right here in Sonora Safari." Danni thought she knew who, but she didn't say.

"Danni, that's a pretty serious accusation," Riley said as he looked straight into Danni's eyes.

"I know," she said quietly, "and I have no real proof, just a gut feeling."

"Well, I'll see what I can find out," Riley said, "don't worry about it. See you Thursday."

Danni went home. She hadn't seen Mary in days. She had heard her moving around late at night, but they hadn't bumped into each other. Today Mary was home. She looked exhausted. The dark circles were back under her eyes. She was sitting at the kitchen table surrounded by her books.

"Where were you all night, Danni," Mary asked.

Danni gave her a glass of iced sun tea and poured one for herself. She thought about changing the subject but went for incomprehensibility instead.

"I wazzat Carson's, she mumbled quietly and rapidly.

"What'd you s--," Mary started to ask and then she got it. "You were?" Her eyes got wide, a look of concern crossed her face.

Mary had learned a lot, Danni thought.

"It'll be OK," Danni said, "I'm going home soon anyway. She changed the subject.

"You going to be here for dinner?" It worked.

"I wasn't really planning to eat," Mary said.

Now the attention was shifted back on Mary.

"Well you look exhausted, you should eat something. I'll fix dinner. We can eat together."

Danni was already in the kitchen pulling things out of the refrigerator. She had decided to make bean and cheese burritos, chimichanga style. She started heating the oil to fry the burritos. Then she shredded the lettuce and cut the tomatoes.

"How are you doing with the studying for the comps," Mary asked.

"We're on hold temporarily because we're going to the National Reading Conference this coming weekend," Danni told her.

Mary had to take the comps in the same subject area next semester. One of her majors was in Early Childhood Education. Danni had promised to leave Mary her notes.

"Geez, the comps are in two weeks, aren't you getting nervous," Mary asked.

Actually Danni was nervous about a lot of things -- comps being the least of her worries. She wasn't doing this college thing quite right this time around. She was worried about her feelings for Carson. She was worried about her theories about Perez's demise, she was getting desperate

168

about how she would get the money to go home and she was near panic about the black ice in the Poconos.

She was supposed to leave for home in a month. A-A and Nicole wanted her to stop in Miami for Christmas before she went north. But she didn't want to bum Mary out with a catalogue of her woes.

"We've really been working hard," was all she said. "I think we're really prepared."

As they ate their dinner Mary thoughtfully asked, "Danielle do you know what you're doing?"

"I haven't a clue," Danni answered. And it was true. But she knew the ride was almost over. And, although, she was sad about leaving and sad about Perez, she no longer felt depressed.

20
Tucson

On Thursday Danielle turned in her key to Sonora Safari, gave a last lingering look at the shabby office, said goodbye to the partners, and closed one chapter of her life in Tucson. Riley didn't say anything about the things Danni had told him and she didn't bring it up again. She hated to leave things unfinished but everyone else seemed to think Perez's funeral had brought previous events to a close. Even though the spirit of the place had already departed it felt strange to close the office door for the last time.

On Friday she left for the convention in San Antonio with Megan and Skye. They headed south in the blue metal palomino in high spirits (figuratively, not literally). They stopped in El Paso and had heuvos rancheros; the best Danni had ever eaten. It felt fine to be in Texas. It wasn't cold there yet, but, for some reason, it was cooler than in the north. There were huge white ranches set back against low hills with split rail or white rail fences around mammoth horse corrals. Mile after mile of scrub country, the same chaparral that Danni had seen on her way to Tucson, rolled past the windows. They took turns driving. They were all on Skye's case. She drove the Toyota with reckless abandon. She was a maniac behind the wheel. Danni needed blinders. The conversation consisted of; "watch out, Skye," "slow down, Skye," "oh no, Skye!"

The more they squealed the faster she drove. There are no state troopers in Texas apparently or perhaps they recognized Skye as a kindred spirit, a true Texan. Danni's intestines were twisted in knots. Wave after wave of cramps in frenetic peristalsis clamored to be eased. How do you tell the stage to slow down when the banditos seem to be gaining? Besides, where do you find a rest station in the wilderness? Finally Danni in desperation scrutinized the landscape rushing past the window beside her. "Here," she screamed, when she saw a pull out next to a camouflaging stand of thin trees with thick low brush underneath, "pull over, stop." Skye had great reflexes. They all had whiplash. Danni knew Skye would torture her for this one.

"I gotta go," Danni said over her shoulder, as she leaped out of the car. She wended her way carefully to the thickest part of the brush. Skye, however, was not Danni's only tormentor. Nature must have had it in for her too. Her first visitors in her helpless position were two quiet deer, both does, who simply stared at her momentarily out of their large, wet, wild-dark eyes and when she registered, left rapidly off stage left. Her next visitors, who she fortunately heard before they came into view, were two dogs and a hunter. Danni did not take time to think. She adjusted her clothing and headed for the dirt drive they had pulled off on, Skye saw her coming. By then the hunter and dogs were in hot pursuit. Skye yelled, "maybe he'll marry you," as she headed off down the road. Anything one might do in such a situation would appear incredibly stupid. Solutions to her dilemma flashed across Danni's mind. She could link arms with the man and say, "Hi Sweetie, what's for dinner." Not her style. She could smile sweetly and just say, "They'll be right back. They just went down the road for some beer," She could go Mae West and say, "My honey, what a big gun you have," but she would have to be willing to accept the consequences. She could try to act professional, "I heard this land was for sale." Or she could do what she did which was not look back. She could run down the shoulder of the highway with her arms waving, yelling, "Skye, I'm going to kill you."

Skye finally came back to get her. That was Skye, full of evil spirits and devilment. Megan and Skye giggled on and off all the way to San Antonio which made things worse. Danni nursed her wounded ego. She still wasn't on the best of terms with them when they pulled up at the St. Anthony.

That hunter could have shot her thinking that he was shooting the deer.

The St. Anthony took Danni's mind off her embarrassment. The hotel was set at the back of a park, which resembled a village green. There was even a cannon in the center with a neat pile of cannonballs. Round globe lamps on old-fashioned lampposts surrounded the square to light the way to the front portico. Two story, arched palladian windows graced the facade. Through the glass Danni could see Victorian-design furniture, Queen Anne chairs and tables, gold brocade fabric, gold carpets, huge fresh flower arrangements and crystal chandeliers. Framed in one vast window was a black grand piano, top down. Danni wanted to see it at night, to walk back through the dark park in the soft evening air when all the globes were lit and the warm golden light spilled out to the low gardens; when the piano top was raised and sweet notes followed the light.

Their room was a bit disappointing; it was neat and attractive, but very small. It didn't matter though, Danni knew they wouldn't be spending much time there. The rest of San Antonio got better and better. After they registered at the conference they took a walk along the river. All along the river walk were the pampered shops and restaurants of loving proprietors. The tree limbs were traced with strings of tiny white lights. It was enchanting. They had to leave it all to go back for the first session of the conference, which was a dinner followed by a speech.

They worked hard at the conference, even Skye. For all her wicked lightheartedness, Skye was a serious student and a good one. They attended different sessions, they compared notes. They went to luncheons and dinners. They got to rub elbows with the authors of their textbooks, the theorists and those with a more practical bent. They heard Walter Kintsch speak, "The Representation of Meaning in Memory." It made them feel brilliant and scholarly. At night they hung out in hospitality suites trying to figure out who was going to

173

be sleeping with who. At the dance on the last night but one they were surrounded by handsome men in suit coats clamoring to dance with them. No cowboys here.

Skye wanted to ask Dr. Alexander and his wife out to dinner.

"He won't want to go," Megan said.

"Well then, he'll say no," Skye answered. So she asked. He said yes. Danni felt shy in this company but she, of course, went along. Skye picked out a place on the river walk, a steak house. Their professor wore a ten gallon hat as if to say, no college cowboys, huh? The hostess seated them in a window bay. It was dusk; the tiny lights glittered through the glass, reflected back from the rippled surface of the dark water. Danni realized that she could get hooked on affluence. All around were people who had money, and they made their world so lovely.

Dr. Alexander was feeling good. He liked this place. Skye was sometimes very astute about people, occasionally slightly obnoxious, but still astute. Danni's ego was still slightly tender from Skye's last character revelations. Dr. Alexander was ordering wine. He called the maitre d' who appeared with a towel draped over his arm. Danni wasn't going to miss this. She didn't hear what he ordered but he was very specific. While the maitre d' got the wine, the professor told them he had discovered this wine last year in Europe and that it was so delicious he had ordered several cases. Danni had shared gallons of Almaden and Gallo at the all-night parties with her colleagues, but she certainly could not claim an educated palate or tongue or whatever. Still she knew what would happen next and she waited with anticipation for the entire scenario to unfold. The wine glasses appeared next to their plates. The silver tray arrived with the wine at room temperature. The cork was removed and pulled delicately across under Dr. Alexander's nose. His mustache twitched. He nodded to the maitre d'. A few centimeters were poured into his glass. He took a tentative sip, nodded again to the maitre d' who then began to fill all their glasses. It wasn't until she heard the expelled air that she realized they had all been holding their breath. The rest of the dinner unfolded with satisfying elegance. The guests warmed to each other. Talk flowed easily. Their faces were flushed. Danni looked at Megan and Skye as they stood up to leave. They were as flushed with their triumph as she was, although Skye still tried to look blasé. Their professor even insisted on paying for the meal. They were all in love with him. He probably knew it. Probably, so did his wife, but she didn't seem worried.

The trio, Megan, Danni and Skye, wandered back across town. They were quiet but elated. They lingered in the lobby for a while listening to the piano man. Then they buzzed off to bed. Comps were one week away. The next day, they high tailed it back to Tucson. They scheduled one more meeting for Thursday evening. Danni dropped them off and drove home. She was more confused than ever. "What do I want out of life," she asked herself. She had always accepted whatever happened as being her life. Now she suspected that some people chose a life and made the world conform. Which world did she want? She certainly knew some she wasn't interested in. She thought it was taking her a long time to grow up.

On Wednesday Danni talked to Kate. She hadn't seen her in ages.

"Danni," she said, "where have you been?"

"Oh geez, Kate, things have been moving pretty fast. Comps are in less than a week you know. And I went with some people to the reading conference in San Antonio. I saw Carson --"

"Yeah, I heard Colleen left," Kate said.

Kate was brutal sometimes. She didn't believe in sugar coating. Danni, of course, liked a little sugar on everything, but she appreciated Kate's honesty.

"Aren't you leaving in a few weeks," Kate asked.

"Yes, I have to but I'm trying to figure out how to get home without driving. And I want to stop in Miami first to see A-A and Nicole," Danni told her.

"Danni," Kate explained patiently, "put a note on the school bulletin board. There are always students looking for rides."

"Good idea," Danni said, "I also think I'll go to the swap meet and sell some of my stuff. I can't take all these things home. I have to get your tape deck back to you. And I want you to have the sling chair if you want it."

"So what about Carson?"

Danni had no idea what to say even though she knew the question was coming.

"Don't worry, Kate, I'm leaving, it'll be OK," Danni said.

Danni realized that she never thought about what she would do if Carson asked her to stay. She knew she couldn't and he wouldn't.

"I'll go to the swap meet with you," Kate said, "talk to you later, Stuart's here."

Danni hadn't even seen their new house yet. Before she left -- one more loose end.

On Thursday Danni put the notice on the bulletin board at school.

"Driver's wanted (not riders)
Going to Miami, then New York"
(Her phone number and name)

She didn't hold out much hope but she offered up one of her selfish little silent prayers. "Dear Lord, please handle this, I'll never ask for another thing." As usual, it seemed true at the time. When she got home from school she looked through the mail. Usually there wasn't a lot. Today Mary was home. She held out an envelope.

"Danni, someone slipped this under the door. I didn't see who. I wasn't home yet."

Danni opened the sealed envelope and read the note. The handwriting was unfamiliar. It was unsigned. Danni's hand with the note dropped to her side. She must have seemed mystified because Mary said, "What is it, Danni? What does it say?"

"This is strange," Danni told Mary. She felt a chill, shivered. It says, "Meet me at Sonora Safari Friday night at 8:00 p.m. I have some information for you."

"Are you going?" Mary asked.

"I might, I shouldn't but I have to know."

"I'll go with you," Mary said, "you can't go there alone that late at night."

"No, I should go alone. I don't want to get you involved in this."

"I'm going and that's that," Mary said with unusual forcefulness.

"OK," Danni said, "I think I would feel better if you were with me."

Danni collected her books and her note cards and got ready to go to the meeting at Megan's. She still had the note in her hand. She tucked it between the pages of one of her books like a bookmark.

Megan's house, as always, was bright and warm and welcoming. They were all a bit panicked; the exam was on Saturday. The boys were still up and José was home. He took them in the family room and read to them. They formed a sweet huddle on the couch. Norman Rockwell time. Oh what I'm missing, Danni thought.

They settled down in front of the living room fireplace. The evening was slightly chilly and Megan had a fire softly burning.

"Let's get organized," Skye said.

Skye said let's get organized, Danni thought, this is serious. They made a list. Each had studied a special area. They would take turns reviewing and drilling the others in those areas. When they had made the list Danni went to the kitchen with Megan to make tea. When they came back Skye was tucking something into a book. Danni looked a question at her. Skye said, "something fell." Danni didn't have long to think about it. They were off till early morning, "Whose theory is blah, blah, blah? When? What practical application? Names, dates, and ideas from scholars they had met and those they had never met marched through the airy room like legions of tired cowpokes. Finally their brains refused to function and the three women unfolded their tired bodies from the floor, carried the accumulated dishes, papers and overflowing ashtrays out to the kitchen, wished each other luck and hugged good night. Danni drove the little blue metal sleeper car home by rote.

On Friday Danni slept late. She scuffed around the apartment in nightgown and flip-flops. She was too nervous to eat. She hauled out the Instant Breakfast from the back of a cupboard. Oh, no, I'm regressing, she thought.

She spread the note cards out on the table and tried to review. She couldn't concentrate. She wandered from room to room picking out what she planned to sell at the swap meet and making a pile of it all on the sling chair in the living room. Tim knocked on the door. She jumped. She hadn't seen him for a while, not since Rachel. She sent him away, sorry she was busy, exams, had to study. Jitzy hormones were not what she needed today.

She hadn't used her health spa membership for a couple of months but she decided that she would go sit in the steam bath for a while. Maybe it would help her relax. It was hard to form thought with all that steam in the air. She paddled across the pool a couple of times, towel dried her hair, threw on her sundress, and went back home.

Mary was home by then, Carson called. Good luck on her test. Maybe they could do something on Sunday.

Danni knew she must be really upset, because that only cheered her up a little bit. She was jumpy. She couldn't sit still.

"Mary, go for a walk with me."

Mary did.

They left the apartment again about 7:30 and drove to Sonora Safari. The store was dark. They waited in the car awhile but nothing happened. At five after eight Danni said, "Let's go in" and got out of the car.

Danni tried the door. It was open. She didn't know what to expect. She hesitated in the doorway. She looked at Mary. Mary took her hand but it didn't help much. Mary's hand was shaking.

"Let's leave," Mary whispered. "I don't like this."

Danni didn't like it either but she was going in. "Wait for me here," she said.

"No way," Mary whispered back. Danni reached for the office light switch. She was surprised when the office lights came on. No one was there, so they tiptoed through to the door into the shop. That door wasn't locked either. With her hand still on the doorknob Danni flipped the switch for the shop lights. This time nothing happened. The shop wasn't totally dark, because it wasn't dark outside yet. There weren't many windows in the shop, though so it wasn't light either. She could make out the shapes of the circular clothing racks. The shelves along the walls, which contained the boots, shoes and various gear were mostly in shadow except those across from the large glass doors on the front of the shop. The counter was right outside the office. She could see behind it from where she stood. There was no one there. Mary still had her other hand and she was tugging on it now, trying to pull Danni back into the office.

"This is crazy, Danni. We should leave. We should have told the police about that note," Mary whispered.

She's right, Danni thought, having had the same thought several times herself, but what would the police have done? The note didn't say anything threatening.

Danni felt scared, but she didn't feel her usual anticipation of imminent death. She had come too far from her initial fragile state this year. It was not that she felt invincible, blind faith in the future was gone forever. It was more an acceptance of inevitability. She was beginning to cast her lot with the folks who said, "when your number is up, it's up, and there's nothing you can do about it." She didn't believe that her number was flashing yet behind the big meat counter in the sky. She didn't hear anyone saying, "who's got number 73," or whatever.

"I'm going in," she said to Mary. "Why don't you stay here, or you could go get the police."

"I'm not leaving you here alone," Mary hissed back.

So Danni advanced slowly into the semi-dark shop with Mary holding on and tiptoeing silently behind her over the concrete floor. When they got to the first clothes rack Danni stopped and put her hand on the circular bar around the top. Mary didn't stop fast enough. She bumped into her.

"Warn me when you're going to stop," Mary told her.

"Sh-h," Danni whispered. "I thought I heard something."

"You did," a very threatening male voice said, "I'm over here."

They both turned toward the voice. Danni recognized Fred by the dim evening light coming through the door. He had a gun, pointed right at them.

"I told you to come alone," Fred said.

Danni ignored that; she couldn't get over that it was Fred standing there, the zero, the blank. She had expected to see someone else altogether. It just wouldn't sink in.

"Fred, what are you doing here, and with a gun. You don't even sound like yourself."

"You never suspected it was me," he said, sounding surprised and a little disappointed. Then you could tell he got used to the idea that he hadn't been a suspect, that he liked the idea. His tone had a new cockiness.

"Yeah, well I guess I did a pretty good job then. I didn't do any of this on purpose anyway," he said. "I started dealin' because I was way over my head in debt -- the wife, the kids, the house, the car. I don't use the stuff -- only except once in a while. But somehow Perez found out I had good stuff -- from Chet maybe. He was strung out on that Gina. She was messin' up his mind. But he took to the stuff, couldn't leave it alone. He was makin' me nervous. How come you smart college girls got yourself involved in this. Guess you're not so smart after all, huh?" he sneered.

Danni wanted to keep him talking so that he wouldn't start doing anything with that gun. "But Fred, you're not in trouble then. If I didn't think it was you, chances are no one else knows anything either. Why don't you just put the gun down and we'll --"

"Stay right where you are, you college bitches. You <u>know</u> now, you think I believe that if I jist let you go you're not gonna tell anyone. Now I gotta finish what I started. Besides I hate you college girls -- always thinkin' you're so great, treatin' the rest of us like science experiments. Let go'a that rack and start walkin'. I'll be right behind you."

Danni knew they had to do what he said, so she looked over at Mary to see how she was doing. She seemed to be doing OK. She looked a little angry, a little pale, but that could be the light. Besides, who knew what Danni looked like. She nodded to Mary and they started walking. She would like to have thought that she could do something heroic like turn fast and karate chop that gun right out of Fred's hand with the hands she and Mary still had clasped together, and then whirl around and kick him in the balls, but physical action was not quite her forté. So she fell back again on language.

"Really Fred, you wouldn't have to serve much time, you'd probably even get probation. After all this is your first conviction, right?"

Fred was quiet. She thought he was listening.

"How could you know Perez would get so depressed and commit suicide like that. They can't blame that on you."

"Keep moving," Fred snarled.

181

They were moving across the length of the store, obviously headed for the loading doors at the back.

Where was he taking them, Danni worried? She was getting nervous now. It looked like he was taking them outside, maybe to the jeep, maybe out in the desert. This time there really might be a body that wouldn't be found for a long time. This time there might be two. How could she have gotten Mary mixed up in all of this? However much she, Danni, might be harboring some secret death wish so she could get it over with and stop worrying about it, Mary didn't seem at all preoccupied with the subject. All her plans and actions showed a readiness to embrace life and enjoy it.

They were near the back door.

"Danni, where is he taking us?" Mary whispered. She was shivering; Danni could feel it through her hand.

"Shuddup and keep movin'," Fred growled.

Danni tried again, "Fred we won't tell a soul about this, don't make it worse. So far the only charge is drug dealing, this will make it murder. You will go to jail for this, for a long time, too."

"Don't you get it, college bitch," Fred said, "I killed him. Perez didn't commit suicide. He was runnin' out of cash, and runnin' out of time. The partners were after him. They knew he was strung out. They knew he was takin' the cash. Perez said he was gonna confess, plead for mercy, and try to make things right. He was gonna tell them about me. I figured it out, he had to. And I'm not even college educated."

Danni was in shock. She realized that Fred was desperate, that unless they did something this really was boot hill, the last roundup, the big rodeo in the sky. Her brain was still functioning, but her body had no self-defense strategies. It had been too long since the cave or the tribe, wherever her ancestry began. Maybe when he tried to get them into the jeep she could try something. Mary must have been thinking along the same lines because she squeezed Danni with her fingers and kept trying to point backwards with their joined hands.

"Break it up. You two, you queer or something? Let go hands," Fred said. He stuck the gun in the ribs on Danni's back. "Hey you, college bitch, open the door, and no funny stuff. Walk straight out. No fancy turns or nothing. Your girlfriend can go right out behind you. Then me, with the gun on her."

Danni did everything exactly like he said. This was no time to take any chances. It was full dark now. There was no moon up although Danni looked at the evening star (which wasn't a star) lovingly since it might be the last time. They crossed to the jeep. Fred kept the gun on Mary so Danni really didn't dare try anything.

"OK. College bitch."

Danni knew he meant her.

"Put your hand on the front door of the jeep, open her up and slide all the way over to the driver's seat. Your girlfriend can sit in back next to me and guess where the gun will --"

Suddenly, there were car headlights all around them and at the same instant someone sprang up and knocked the gun out of Fred's hands. Someone else yanked his hands behind him and put on handcuffs. An official voice said, 'You have the right to remain silent,' and kept going.

Danni couldn't believe it was over at first. She started shaking. She was dazed. She bent her knees and made a lap to put her head in. When she felt steadier she got up and looked around her.

"What? How'd you know?" Danni said, still dazed, and then she saw Skye with, of all people, Carson and Riley.

"Ohmigod, you saw the note, didn't you Skye? That was what you were putting back in my book. But Carson, how'd you get here. Do you two know each other?" She was still shivering.

Carson held her then and Skye put her arm on Mary's shoulder.

"No, I called Kate, she gave me the number," Skye said. "I remembered you talking about Kate when she got her degree. Danni, what were you thinking of? You better get your act together, girl."

Now that Danni was safe, she started trembling like crazy and crying and hiccuping. Carson held her tighter and rubbed her back. "He killed Perez," she said, "I never even imagined that. The way Perez was I believed he did it to himself."

"We knew," Riley said, back from wherever he had disappeared to. I've had my eyes on old Fred for a while now. We were ready to move in. You almost screwed things up. Now you two have to come downtown and make a statement."

"You'll stay with me tonight," Carson said.

"No, I don't want Mary to stay alone," Danni said.

"I'll stay with Mary," Skye said.

"Geez, we have our exam tomorrow. How're we ever going to pass?" Danni moaned.

"Com'on everyone, let's get going," Riley said.

Danni climbed into the Ford truck with Carson. Mary rode in Skye's current vehicle, borrowed from one of her many male friends. It was late when they finished at the police station. They told Danni that they thought they had enough evidence without her testimony but they'd fly her back out to Tucson if they needed her as a witness. Danni found Riley, thanked him, and said good bye.

"Stay outta trouble," he called after her.

"No problem," Danni shouted back, "and, at that moment, she really meant it.

Carson held her all through the rest of the night. Danni's emotions were so churned up she didn't think she'd be able to get to sleep, but she was exhausted and felt so safe that Carson was nuzzling her awake with kisses on her neck before she even knew she had slept. Danni left for her exam with the languorous eyes of a recently satisfied woman. When Carson left her off at the college he said he'd call her about Sunday. "Do good now," he called after her.

Her hormones got her through half the exam, her involvement with the exam itself got her through the rest. But she wasn't sure how she had done on it. Now that it was over, her feelings flooded in. Relief was there but also a bad case of the blues. Megan and Skye were waiting for her in the lobby. Megan took her shoulders and looked in her eyes. "You OK, Danni?" she asked.

"No," Danni cried, and Megan did what any mom would do. She gathered Danni in and comforted her. Danni stepped back, gave Megan a smile, and with her hand still on Megan's shoulder asked Skye how Mary was doing.

"Mary's doing fine. She's worried about you. She's a pretty strong lady. Let's go get a beer."

"Good idea," Megan said.

They walked to a college bar a few blocks away from the campus. It had picnic tables on the front lawn under a pergola. Skye got a pitcher and some glasses. Megan and Danni found a place to sit. The place was crowded. They weren't the only ones who had finished exams.

While Skye was setting down the pitcher and the glasses she told Danni that the police had called her place last night to tell her that they would drive her car over to North Swan Road and leave it there for her. Megan said she would take her home. They didn't know what else to say to each other now that everything was almost over.

"So, Danni you leave next weekend, huh?" Skye asked. "Why don't you stay?"

"I can't," Danni said, "the school already sent a letter confirming the end of the sabbatical. They expect me back in the classroom at the beginning of the spring semester. They will prosecute if I try to break the agreement. Something tells me they've run into this before."

"Well, Dan, we'll miss you," Megan said.

"Me too," Danni said in a small voice.

The pitcher was gone, the blues were back. Megan took Danni home towards the mountains on North Swan Road, home to the little blue metal battle veteran and the little green lizard.

On Sunday she said her good-byes to Carson. He wouldn't let her get soupy but she did tell him that he was a good person to know in a crisis. He reached behind the seat when he left her at her apartment and pulled out his own ten-gallon hat, big, heavy, suede, which he placed on her head.

"Thanks, Carson," Danni said truly pleased, then she leaned over and kissed him deeply one last time.

"I'll write to you," he said.

"You don't know my address," Danni said, walking alongside the truck as he started to pull away.

"I'll get it from Kate," he said.

Danni waved. She had tears in her eyes.

"Bye," said Cowboy Bob, with exactly the same twang she had heard on that very first phone call. Cowboys are obviously not big on protracted good-byes.

Now a great blue funk really took hold. Not only was Danni still nervous from her recent brush with "real" death, but it was obvious that she actually was going home. The money for the trip had arrived from her parents before the fateful events of late last week. Her blue desert trekker had been tuned up and fed oil for colder climes. She was going to the swap meet on Tuesday to sell her worldly goods. She was having lunch with Kate one last time on Thursday at the new house she shared with Stuart.

However, she still didn't have any drivers to get her home. The icy Poconos were once again looming large in her overactive imagination. Danni's knees quivered every time she thought of driving home alone. It was not her intent to malign the lovely honeymoon spots of Pennsylvania. She knew her fear was irrational. After what she had been through, she suspected she was a survivor. She had also inherited a grassroots awareness of such pithy truths as "the way over an obstacle is through it." But Danni had lost her faith in physics; she no longer trusted things like gravity or centripetal force. Depression gone, the bone deep knowledge that death can happen would never leave. And she knew she couldn't drive alone through the Poconos.

Something or someone was watching out for her, Danni concluded, because the impossible happened. On Monday afternoon a guy named Anatole called. He sounded nice; he had a slight European accent and a valid driver's license. He was a senior at the university. He was going to Miami and New York over the Christmas break. "Would she be coming back?" he asked. No. OK, he could fly back. Yes, he could leave on Friday.

Then on Tuesday morning a guy named Jerry called. He was a freshman, from New York City. (She had recognized the brash dialect instantly.) He had a mother in Miami and a father in New York City. Danni felt bad to be this pleased by the climbing divorce rates, but she couldn't help herself just this once. Two drivers! She would make it. And she'd get to see A-A and Nicole too.

She left for the swap meet in her little blue peddler's cart with a lighter heart than she had had in weeks. The swap meet was in a big empty parking lot covered with dirt and gravel. You rented a spot and set up shop in your own little space. Some people sold new merchandise: T-shirts, jeans, cowboy hats of all descriptions. There were lots of jewelers who made their own very beautiful southwestern jewelry, silver with stones of coral, lapis, turquoise, malachite. And there were also lots of jewelers who sold less beautiful, and less expensive, retail versions of southwestern jewelry. And then there were people like Danni, who just staged an al fresco garage sale. Danni had made some of her best buys at the swap meet. Now she needed to convert some of these goods back into cash. Like people at garage sales, people at swap meets are not big spenders if they can help it. She knew she wasn't going to go away rich.

While Danni was busy passing out the memorabilia of her year in Tucson for various amounts of small change, Kate arrived. She helped Danni with the customers for a while and then, when the cassette tapes were gone, things started to quiet down.

"Geez Kate, it was nice of you to come," Danni finally got to say.

"No big deal," Kate said. "I was worried about you. Carson told Stuart and me what happened."

"Oh, he did?"

"Danni, you could have been killed. I hope you'll start being more careful about people when you get home."

Danni had to admit to herself that she didn't always exercise real good judgment in her choice of companions, but sometimes her instincts were great and she reminded Kate of that.

Kate got it right away. Not all college girls are dense. "Thanks Danni, that's a nice thing to say," she said.

"I got two drivers," Danni told her, "can you believe that?"

"They're both going to Miami and New York?" Kate said incredulously.

"Yeah, amazing, huh?" Danni beamed back at Kate over her shoulder.

"I'm glad for you Danni, I know you've been dreading the trip, but aren't you a little homesick?"

Actually, putting all else aside, Danni had to admit she was. And that she couldn't wait to see A-A and Nicole.

Kate went to the food trailer and got them some snacks. She stayed around and chatted and helped Danni sell for a couple of hours. There wasn't exactly a crowd beating its way to Danni's cash box. After a while Kate gave Danni a hug, said she'd see her Thursday for lunch and went home to her new life. For about the eightieth time since Danni met her, she wished Kate could meet A-A and Nicole. Maybe someday.

While she sat there melting at the swap meet she thought back over all the people she had met in Tucson that she would miss. She looked in front of her at the mountains and the desert colors and drank it all in one last time in what she knew would be one of her last peaceful moments here. Finally she straightened up with a sigh, packed the few things that were left and headed home to start packing. She had made forty dollars and a few odd cents.

On Wednesday she stopped at Megan's house. She didn't have any extra cash but she wanted to leave her something special. She decided to give Megan, Skye and Mary some of the pottery glasses and cups made for her by her good friend from her earlier college days, Jackie. Megan wasn't home and Danni was sort of relieved. This goodbye stuff was getting old. She left the two labeled packages on the front steps right in front of the door.

On Wednesday afternoon Yellow Freight came by as arranged and picked up most of her stuff. There was no room for most of her possessions in the blue metal passenger coach.

On Thursday she put the sling chair and the tape player in the back of Stuart's Ford which Kate had borrowed for the day and went off to have lunch at Kate's. Stuart wasn't at home when they got there but he stopped by later for a beer. It was sort of a lackadaisical conversation. Danni realized she hadn't known these two for very long, but they were still very special. Danni wanted to stay in touch. Kate wrote her new address and phone number and her Mom's number in New Paltz in Danni's phone book. Danni reciprocated. Kate would give her a call when she visited her Mom this summer. They climbed back in the Ford and Kate drove her back to the apartment. She gave Danni a hug and a kiss on the cheek.

"Take care," she said, as she drove off.

Danni sat forlornly on the white cast iron patio chair with her elbows leaning on the table and her chin resting on her hands. God it was hard to leave here, a year wasn't enough. Life is so understated, most of it happens in a nonverbal, a priori corner of our mind.   There was no way to express how it all really made her feel in any way that was socially acceptable in the 70's, now that tearing of hair and rending of clothing was considered out of fashion.   It didn't matter, everything was wrapped up here, all the loose ends neatly cut or tied off.   Even Kate had traded in her carefree single hacienda by the mountains for the stability of a more conventional middle class ranch home with a landscaped yard.

Realizing how foolish she was getting Danni got up and went inside. Mary was keeping the place. She wasn't done with school until June so her stuff was still around, but all Danni's paintings and trinkets were riding in the back of the Yellow Freight. She didn't live here anymore.

Mary came yawning out of her bedroom, just up from a nap. "Let's go eat at the Smuggler's Inn," she said. "I'm buying."

"I have enough, you don't have to buy, but I agree, let's go," Danni said. She certainly didn't want to sit around here babysitting her nerves.

"No, I'm paying," said Mary firmly, continuing the ridiculous age old argument that people will still be having at the edge of future time. Danni gave in and went to get gussied up. Another goodbye, another person who would never probably know the depth of Danni's feelings about her.

Friday morning old blue was saddled up and ready to go. Danni drove to Jerry's and picked him up. Then they drove to Anatole's to pick him up and headed East on I 10 towards Texas.

21
The Southern Route:
Texas to Florida

Danielle drove first. She wanted to get to know these two before they started driving. She also didn't want to just sit. Her sadness would not allow it. She had the ten-gallon hat perched on her head. Actually it came down to her eyebrows. It was a bit large, but she was indulging herself in some maudlin sentimentality. If she couldn't have Tucson at least she had the hat.

Her corral gate was open and her emotions were out on the range. Along with her sense of loss was a glimmer of excitement, like the tips of trees at the rim of a canyon. She would be with A-A and Nicole for Christmas.

She was using the interviewing skills on her two riders that she had learned from A-A and Nicole. Perhaps that was what made her remember how it was with the three of them. Nicole's interviewing skills were honed mainly in retail stores. She never kept anything. She was always returning items. The zipper was slightly crooked, the buttonholes were just a bit off, the seam was sloppy. She shopped at budget stores but expected hand-made quality. She had never accepted the recent slippage in the quality of ready-to-wear clothing. So she was dogged in her quest for refunds. The main goal was to not get stuck with a due bill.

A-A's interviewing skills were perfected on the phone. They were designed to get maximum information in minimum time. She talked real low; you could never overhear her. Danni could never figure out how the person on the other end knew what she was saying. But when she got off the phone she had the whole scoop about whatever. Danni never had any questions about any event A-A had covered that A-A couldn't answer. A-A never had to say, "oh, I forgot to ask that."

Their techniques are very similar. If you shoot out the questions real fast people will oblige by answering. Don't give them time to make judgments about whether the question is rude or too private. Speed and directness were the two prerequisites to a successful interview. But you also had to care about finding out because you had to think of all these great questions really fast. With friends you were gentle but persistent, with salesgirls you pulled out all the stops. Danni's skills had never caught up with the masters'. She got due bills more often than refunds. A-A always came up with something Danni had neglected to ask. Maybe she just couldn't care enough. However, she focused what paltry skills she had on her two relief stagecoach drivers as if the gold shipment delivery depended on it.

Anatole was sitting next to her, Jerry in the back, although Jerry was already complaining about the cramping in his legs, and that he should have the front seat. Since he was the most vocal Danielle started with him.

"Where did you grow up, Jerry?" she asked.

"Queens."

Before he could elaborate, "you lived there all your life?"

"Yeah, my parents were born there."

"How did you end up in Tucson?"

"My older brother goes to school here; he hates winter, loves the school, so I came too."

"Why didn't you catch a ride home with him?"

"He had to stay to do a paper, make up an incomplete."

"What year is he in?"

"He's a junior."

"So who's in Florida?" Danni asked, although she already knew the answer.

"My mom, she and my dad split up about three years ago. She likes sunshine too, must run in the family," Jerry said.

"Let's switch," he whined, "it's really killin' my legs back here. Com'on, Anatole, you're short."

"In a while," Danni told him. Anatole said nothing.

"What's your major?" Danni continued her interrogation, as if no interruption had occurred.

"Haven't decided yet, I'm in liberal arts for now."

"So you just graduated from high school last year?" Danni asked. She wanted to get some idea how old he was. He looked and acted pretty young.

"Yeah, in June." He stretched his legs out across the back seat, accompanied by isometric lifts and groans, until they rested on top of the armrest on the other side.

Danni started on Anatole who had said two words since he got in the car, the two words being "hello" and "certainly" when Danni told him to stow his bag in the trunk. He seemed calm and mature.

"How about you, Anatole? Where'd you grow up," Danni asked.

"Brooklyn," he answered calmly with his slight European accent.

"Were you born there?"

"No, Lithuania, my parents came when I was two," he told her; "they separated when I was nine and I've lived back and forth between New York and Florida ever since. I'm thirty-four, I'm 5' 11", and I'm an architecture major," he said, with a wry smile that suggested he knew what she was up to.

And so they drove through Texas, with Jerry grousing and complaining and telling them more than they ever wanted to know about his family, and Anatole who was obviously somewhat irritated by Jerry, smiling at Danni and occasionally throwing a dry, sarcastic barb with his calm voice towards Jerry in the back seat. Jerry, of course, either didn't get his drift or had decided to ignore him.

After about four hours they switched drivers and Jerry drove for a while. Danni sat in back. Jerry wasn't a great driver but Anatole watched him like a hawk. Danni suggested that Anatole take a snooze since he had to drive next, but Anatole said he didn't plan to sleep at all and Danni decided not to argue with him. After that Danni fell asleep and slept without guilt all the rest of the way to Florida. She slept like she had been drugged. She had decided to trust these two. She woke up twice after that, once when Anatole took over as driver, and she poked her head up once when she heard them "discussing" the incredible amount of development going on in Houston. After that she slept all the way to the Florida Panhandle.

They stopped for breakfast at a motel dining room in the Florida Panhandle. Anatole wanted lots of coffee. Danni wanted to wash her face, put on fresh make up and maybe spend the rest of the trip in an upright position. At the breakfast table she looked at her two companions. Jerry had dark, deeply tanned skin. He had thick dark hair parted on the left side, not too long, not too short, and thick brown eyebrows to match. He looked very young. He was about 6' 2", big-boned, medium-built, muscular, and hyperactive.

Anatole, at first, seemed bland, almost mousy. He was short compared to Jerry and very slender. By contrast his coloring was pale. He had no tan; his naturally light-colored skin had obviously been in the library more often than in the sun. His hair color, a dirty blond, also contributed to his generally nondescript appearance. However, on closer inspection, it became apparent that he also was quite attractive in his own way. His hair could have been quite long or fairly short, it was difficult to tell because it was naturally very curly. His face, which seemed expressionless at first, actually revealed sensitivity, intelligence, strength and occasionally a twist of ironic humor. In fact, she decided, he was quite an interesting man and she found herself liking him.

When they left the restaurant it was four in the morning. A thick, white fog blanketed everything. Danni was nervous, but the fog didn't seem to upset Anatole. Danni made Jerry sit in back, even though it meant they would have to listen to more of his whining. She wanted to stay awake and keep an eye on this fog. Anatole had been awake for about twenty hours now and had been driving for about ten. She felt two of them driving, one with a steering wheel, one without, would foil Fate's plans, if he had any. They did get lost once and they cut the U-turn too sharply and drove up on a curb, but after that things went smoothly. The fog burned off around 8:00, or they just rode out of it. In eight hours they were in Miami.

Anatole asked for directions to Nicole's. A-A and Johnnie were coming there too, for Christmas. Danni had talked to Nicole. She knew where to get off I 95. Nicole's house was only a few blocks east of the exit. Anatole blew the horn as they drove into the driveway. Suddenly there they all were, piling out the front door; Nicole with her sophisticated self, David, handsome as ever, A-A, red hair flying and a tall skinny blond kid who must be Johnnie. Danni couldn't hug everybody enough. She loved these guys.

Danni introduced Jerry and Anatole. Everyone said hi. David got her bags out of the car and they all went in the house. Jerry and Anatole took turns calling their moms while Nicole, A-A, and Danielle retired to the living room and started yakking their heads off; blonde, brunette and red heads, bobbing up and down, hands flying through the air. They had to pull Danni out of the fray to get her to drive them home.

When she got back David had left to visit some friends overnight so he wouldn't interrupt the reunion. It felt so good to be here. Nicole and David rented this place and it was great; huge living room, dining room and kitchen in front; and, down the hall off the living room, four bedrooms each with a bath, ending, in the back, with a huge master bedroom and another bath. Along this bedroom wing corridor was also a set of sliding glass doors out to the patio by the pool. The pool and patio were surrounded by tall white stucco castellated walls. Nicole had red plants in hanging baskets. She had a Christmas cactus covered with red blooms sitting on a bench by an expanse of white wall. It didn't look anything like any Christmas landscape Danni remembered except for the fact that everything was white, red and green.

There was a Christmas tree in the living room. They talked and ate all at once and constantly, sitting on the couch in front of the Christmas tree, until four in the morning. Johnnie was waiting for Santa so he willingly went to bed early. At four they decided that if Johnnie was like most kids on Christmas he would give them about two hours to sleep. A-A promised she'd make him hold out for four.

When they reassembled at the tree with bleary eyes, Danni couldn't help but smile. Johnnie had the same huge, shining eyeballs you see on any child on Christmas morning. As he tore into his gifts the three friends made their exchanges at a more leisurely pace, with cups of coffee, and bagels and cream cheese, snapshots, and exclamations between each gift. Johnnie didn't care how long they took; he was absorbed with his gifts.

Nicole didn't plan to make a big dinner, but Danni couldn't stand to let Christmas go by without a turkey. Besides this was the closest Danni had been to anyone who felt like family in a year. So they passed the hat and Danni went to get a turkey and all the trimmings. When it was stuffed and basted and covered with its own little foil tent, Danni tucked it into the oven, threw on her bathing suit and moved on out to the patio to sleep in the sun with the other two. Johnnie swam, buzzed around them taking snapshots, and generally made the nuisance of himself that any ten-year-old with no playmates would make, until Danni couldn't take it anymore. She took him in the house with her to help her peel potatoes. By the time they set the table, mashed the potatoes, scooped out the turkey and aroused the bathing beauties David was back. They all sat down to eat their Christmas dinner on the patio by the pool. Danni loved the paradoxes and she loved the company. She couldn't stop smiling.

Danni could eat fairly well by now except when she was really nervous. Then her throat would close up again to remind her once again of our evanescent existence. Right now she wasn't having any trouble at all.

While Danni was in Florida she visited every watery spot she could find and, of course, there were plenty. They walked by the ocean, fished in the ocean, ate conch soup down in the Keys. Danni reveled in the salty damp tang of the coastal air. She went to see A-A and Johnnie's trailer in Homestead. Homestead was nice, very rural. She went to the Everglades to see the alligators, A-A's beloved blue herons and the white herons. The sleep she had saved up on the trip to Florida she now squandered in the delight of warm friendship. They were never in bed before three o'clock in the morning, often after.

Then it was time to go. It was time to pick up Jerry and Anatole and face the little blue veteran Toyota towards the terror of the Poconos and the longed for welcome of home.

Danni waved and cried, waved and yelled good-bye until she was halfway down the street and waving at strangers. She had a perfect picture in her mind of the little group she had left standing and waving in Nicole's front yard. She put the ten-gallon hat back on her head. It weighted her down, kept her grounded. It made her feel better in the same way that listening to the blues when you're blue lifts your spirits. Two negatives equal a positive?

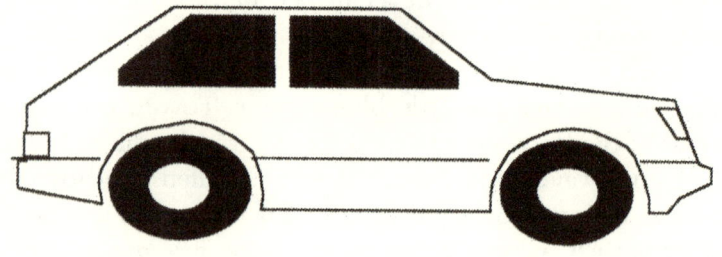

22
Miami to Syracuse:
Through the Poconos

Jerry, who had obviously celebrated a bit too enthusiastically, was actually happy to settle down in the back seat. He adopted the fetal position, which was the only way he could get most of his long body on that small back seat. He hugged the pillow, tossed around a few times, and he was out. He snored.

Anatole drove and he and Danni talked quietly through the morning. The weather was perfect and the forecast looked good. There was no snow in the East and no snow or ice or rain or any other kind of precipitation expected.

"How was your mom?" Danni asked Anatole.

"Oh, she's doing fine," he said, "she spent the whole time cooking and saying the Lithuanian equivalent of eat, eat. So now I feel like a stuffed boy who can hardly move. But my father will take care of that. He never has anything to eat at all. Everyday he says, son, let's do deli."

"Isn't it odd, how our parents never treat us like we're grown up, no matter how old we get?"

"Well, they do and they don't," Anatole said. "I think it's harder for them to let you go when you're their only child."

"My parents have four kids and my mom still babies every one of us. My dad's not as bad."

"Well, I think I like it," Anatole said, "I guess it's like any lifelong habit. The pattern of being a nurturer is difficult to break. Actually, my mother and I talk together like adults; it's usually at the dinner table that I become her little one again. I believe it would be a big problem if I was home all the time. I would be as big as a condominium."

Danni laughed. "I know what you mean," Danni said.

Jerry snorted from the back seat. Danni and Anatole looked at each other and laughed. To their credit, they laughed quietly, but Jerry woke up. He didn't seem to have heard them.

"Where are we," he said like someone who's afraid he's overslept and missed his bus stop.

"We're at the bottom of North Carolina," Anatole told him. "We have a long way to go."

"Well, when we get to Harrisburg, I want to get out. I'll hitch from there," he said.

"That's a good idea," Anatole said, "I guess I'll go with you."

"Sure," Jerry said, "no problem." But he didn't sound thrilled.

Danni panicked. She hadn't even imagined they would separate. Obviously this made sense, geographically speaking. But Danni's fear didn't know from geography, or care for that matter. Could she brave the Poconos alone? It wasn't supposed to snow or rain, but darkness wouldn't be acceptable either.

Danni pleaded with Anatole all through North Carolina, and Virginia. She pleaded while he drove; she pleaded when they stopped to eat. Jerry took over the driving for a while and then Danni really went to work on poor Anatole. How could he leave just before the mountains?

Anatole was patient. "Danni," he argued, "they aren't even very big mountains. The weather is good."

"The weather could change at any moment," Danni moaned. She was shameless. She knew her mindless stubborn terror would paralyze her. She'd have to stay in Harrisburg forever.

"Anatole," she begged, "just come to Syracuse with me. I'll put you on a plane for New York City when we get there. I'll pay your way."

He was adamant; "you can do it, Danni. Syracuse is out of my way. I have too little time left for a good visit with my father and I will not accept plane fare. There are only about five hours of driving left. You're capable of finishing without me."

She was petrified, but she could see that more discussion was useless.

Her throat locked in a stranglehold of constricted muscle tissue. She dropped them off near the Harrisburg exit ramp.

"It was nice meeting you, Jerry, Anatole. Good luck in school next semester," Danni said as she handed their luggage from the trunk. "I hope you get a ride."

"You can do this," Anatole said.

She watched them walk off down the exit ramp. They walked backwards for a bit and waved. Then they put out their thumbs and concentrated on the cars coming off the ramp.

Danni was angry at Anatole at first. She sat there by the exit ramp and steamed for a while. Then she accepted the inevitable, looked for a break in the traffic and faced the Poconos. She turned up the radio; when she could tune in Scranton, the Poconos would be behind her. She gripped the wheel with white knuckles and swallowed with difficulty. But she could not drive with this tension for long. The rhythm of the road started to take over. Her panic was still there but it assumed more reasonable proportions.

Of course fear returned when she entered the mountains, alone in her blue metal ski lift, a sacrifice to the suicidal curves, the breathtakingly deep gorges, the vacuum suck of the tractor trailers, the wobbly grooves scored into the highway (on purpose). It didn't matter; there was no choice but to keep going.

She thought over all the past experiences that had come back to haunt and torment her at this one particular juncture in her life and this highway. She thought she had been very brave, gained immeasurable strength through change and bold action. Hadn't she traveled 2,000 miles, earned a Master's degree, made new friends, stood up to a criminal, and lived through a broken heart without breaking. Hadn't she made it past her depression? She wasn't suicidal anymore; she knew, in fact, that she never really had been. She was in life again, interested in it again, immersed in it again. But here was this fear, still clutching at her throat. As she drove along she came to understand that she would never again live life with the same old unconscious bravado. Life's dangers were real; we are all at risk, but we have to keep on anyway.

I'm more afraid of dying than I am of what comes after, Danni thought as she drove along. Analyzing her fears as she drove seemed to help calm her. "I believe in all alternatives, except hell. Maybe reincarnation; maybe heaven; perhaps molecules decomposing and resynthesizing; or Wordsworth-- we're just fertilizer for new plant growth so the whole cycle can go on and on. I'm not afraid of what comes after life. I'm nervous about pain, violence, horrible disease, murder, and the terrible suspense of not knowing where, when or how. I'm worried about leaving this life which is so miserable, so intriguing, and so real. I want to die peacefully or bravely, after a full, productive life. Will I be brave when the time comes? Can I prepare myself ahead of time? Will I always be this afraid?

There are babies born addicted to heroin, parents who can't feed themselves or their children, people who can't read or write, people who live with no hope. Just grow up and get on with it," she thought. And by then she was through the Poconos, almost to Binghamton and it all looked so familiar and wonderful.

As she drove to her parent's house in the little blue Toyota she thought that maybe she could strike a compromise between freedom and loneliness, between the fear of dying and the joy of living. "I'm back," she said to the molecules of Syracuse air surrounding her.

ACKNOWLEDGEMENTS with gratitude for reprint permission:

"Desperado"
By Don Henley & Glen Frey
©1973 Cass County Music/Red Cloud Music (BMI)
ALL RIGHTS RESERVED

Mammas Don't Let Your Babies Grow Up To Be Cowboys
Words and Music by Ed Bruce and Patsy Bruce
Copyright © 1975 Sony/ATV Songs LLC
All Rights Administered by Sony/ATV Music Publishing,
8 Music Square West, Nashville, TN 37203
International Copyright Secured   All Rights Reserved

BORN TO BE WILD
Words and Music by Mars Bonfire
©Copyright 1968 Universal-MCA Music Publishing, Inc.
a division of Universal Studios, Inc. (BMI)
International Copyright Secured   All Rights Reserved

Thank you to Apple Computer, Inc. for the use of the clip art graphics from the AppleWorks 5 Library. Graphics from AppleWorks are found on the following pages: 12, 18, 38, 46, 52, 74, 110, 162 and 198.

About The Author

NL Brisson is like many other people who were born right after WW II. Her world was shifted by the 'tectonic' cultural upheaveals of the 60's and 70's: rock and roll, the Vietnam war, the Civil Rights Movement, the Women's Lib Movement, and Woodstock (to mention just a few). You can see some of the contradictions caused by the rift between the 50's and 60's in her work.

NL is the second daughter of eight children from a loving family with a blue collar background. She had a good fortune to become the first person in her family to earn a master's degree. She then had the additional good fortune to teach adult education for many years. She lives in Syracuse, NY.